GOD'S GRACEFUL GUIDANCE

A Thematic Approach to Biblical Wisdom for Everyday Life

A collection of scriptures by **Tonya Truster**

Originally Published March 1, 2024
by LGLG Publishing House
Raymore, MO

Library of Congress Cataloging-in-Publication Data

The Cataloging-in-Publication Data for *God's Graceful Guidance: A Thematic Approach to Biblical Wisdom for Everyday Life* is on file at the Library of Congress.
ISBN: 979-8-218-37990-2 (PB)

Concept, Curation, Content and Editing by Tonya Truster
Cover Design and Layout by Brett McGuire: bmcguiredesign.com
Proofreading by Amy Naas
Printed in the United States of America

DEDICATION

With deepest reverence and gratitude, I dedicate this book first and foremost to the Lord Jesus Christ, whose divine hand has authored scriptures that calm all of life's storms. Through His graceful guidance, these verses have been a wellspring of inspiration for me, sustaining me through trials and tribulations.

To my beloved daughters, Lauren and Gabrielle, who were the inspiration behind creating this thematic approach to Biblical wisdom for everyday life. As I watched you embark on your journey to college, my heart yearned for you to have a steadfast anchor in scripture amid life's storms. In curating this collection of verses, my hope is to provide you with a guiding light, offering solace and strength as you navigate life's challenges.

To my husband, Mitch, your steadfast love and unwavering support have been the cornerstone of my aspirations. Your encouragement has breathed life into this dream of publishing, turning mere aspirations into tangible reality.

And to you, dear reader, this book is offered as a beacon of hope and a reservoir of strength, organized by topics to aid you in moments of struggle. Each verse is a testament to God's promises, a prayer to uplift and present before Him in times of adversity.

ACKNOWLEDGEMENTS

Special thanks to Brett McGuire who brought my vision to life. Thank you for your dedication and craftsmanship. Your insights, expertise, and attention to detail have enriched this book beyond measure. Your creative graphic designs, feedback, guidance, and professionalism were invaluable and ensured this book became a reality.

To my beloved husband, Mitch, your love and encouragement have been the driving force behind the realization of this project. Your support sustained me through every challenge, and I am deeply grateful God has blessed me with such an amazing partner in life, and I am immensely proud to be your wife.

To my cherished daughters, Lauren and Gabrielle, your inspiration and understanding during the creation of this book have been invaluable. Your belief in me gave me the strength to persevere, and I am immensely proud to be your mom.

To my dear friends, whose support and encouragement lifted me up when doubts clouded my mind. A special thanks to DeAnn Keith for always being the voice in my ear to publish this book. Your belief in me and this endeavor gave me the courage to press on, and I am forever grateful for your friendship.

Each of you has played a crucial role in bringing this book to fruition, and I am deeply grateful for your contributions. May your kindness and support be forever cherished within the pages of this work.

With heartfelt gratitude,
Tonya Truster

TABLE OF CONTENTS

ANGER

Anger, a God-given emotion, holds immense power within the human experience that we all have struggled with at times. However, its expression demands discernment and restraint. Within the pages of scriptures found in Proverbs, Ephesians, James, Psalms and Ecclesiastes, we find invaluable guidance on managing anger. These verses advocate for the transformative potential of a gentle response, caution against the perils of unchecked rage, and emphasize the virtues of patience and forgiveness. As we delve into these teachings, let us harness their wisdom to navigate the complexities of anger and cultivate inner peace.

I encourage you to pray for God's graceful guidance as you read, meditate on, and memorize the chosen scripture revealed to you by the Holy Spirit.

Proverbs 15:1
¹A soft answer turneth away wrath: but grievous words stir up anger.

Ephesians 4:26
²⁶Be ye angry, and sin not: let not the sun go down upon your wrath.

Proverbs 22:24
²⁴Make no friendship with an angry man; and with a furious man thou shalt not go.

Proverbs 16:32
³²He that is slow to anger is better than the mighty; and he that ruleth his spirit than he that taketh a city.

James 1:19-20
¹⁹Wherefore, my beloved brethren, let every man be swift to hear, slow to speak, slow to wrath: ²⁰For the wrath of man worketh not the righteousness of God.

Proverbs 14:17
¹⁷He that is soon angry dealeth foolishly: and a man of wicked devices is hated.

Proverbs 19:11
¹¹The discretion of a man deferreth his anger; and it is his glory to pass over a transgression.

Psalm 37:3-9
³Trust in the LORD, and do good; so shalt thou dwell in the land, and verily thou shalt be fed. ⁴Delight thyself also in the LORD; and he shall give thee the desires of thine heart. ⁵Commit thy way unto the LORD; trust also in him; and he shall bring it to pass. ⁶And he shall bring forth thy righteousness as the light, and thy

judgment as the noonday. [7]Rest in the LORD, and wait patiently for him: fret not thyself because of him who prospereth in his way, because of the man who bringeth wicked devices to pass. [8]Cease from anger, and forsake wrath: fret not thyself in any wise to do evil. [9]For evildoers shall be cut off: but those that wait upon the LORD, they shall inherit the earth.

Ecclesiastes 7:9
[9]Be not hasty in thy spirit to be angry: for anger resteth in the bosom of fools.

Ephesians 4:31-32
[31]Let all bitterness, and wrath, and anger, and clamour, and evil speaking, be put away from you, with all malice: [32]And be ye kind one to another, tenderhearted, forgiving one another, even as God for Christ's sake hath forgiven you.

Proverbs 29:11
[11]A fool uttereth all his mind: but a wise man keepeth it in till afterwards.

A collection of scriptures by **Tonya Truster**

NOTES

_____
_____
_____
_____
_____
_____
_____
_____
_____
_____
_____
_____
_____
_____
_____
_____
_____
_____
_____
_____
_____
_____
_____
_____
_____
_____
_____
_____

ANGER

NOTES

A collection of scriptures by **Tonya Truster**

NOTES

_____
_____
_____
_____
_____
_____
_____
_____
_____
_____
_____
_____
_____
_____
_____
_____
_____
_____
_____
_____
_____
_____
_____
_____
_____
_____
_____

ANGER

Bible Numerology

Biblical numerology is a fascinating aspect of interpreting scripture that delves into the symbolic meaning of numbers found throughout the Bible. In the pages of the Old and New Testaments, numbers are not just mathematical figures but carry significant spiritual and earthly implications. Each number is infused with symbolic significance, offering insights into God's divine plan and His interactions with humanity.

From the unity represented by the number one to the divine completeness of three, biblical numbers signify various aspects of creation, redemption, and spiritual truths. For instance, the number seven denotes completeness and spiritual perfection, while eight signifies new beginnings and new creations. Each number carries a distinct message, providing a deeper understanding of God's work in the world.

Through biblical numerology, we uncover connections between earthly events and spiritual truths, highlighting God's intricate design and His communication with humanity. From the resurrection symbolized by three to the victory represented by seventeen, each number enriches our understanding of God's purposes and His plan for redemption. As we explore the significance of biblical numbers, we gain deeper insights into the mysteries of God's Word and His divine nature.

I encourage you to seek God's graceful guidance
as you read, meditate on, and study the numerology
present in God's Word, as revealed to you
by the Holy Spirit.

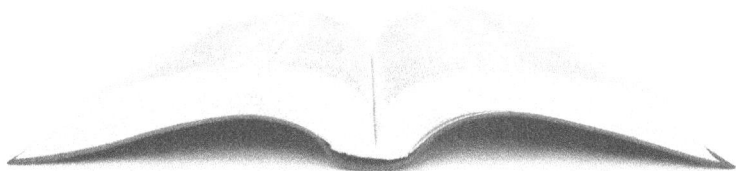

BIBLE NUMEROLOGY

1	Unity	36	Enemy
2	Union, Division, Witnessing	37	Word of God, Exaltation
3	Resurrection, Divine Completeness, Perfection, Godhead, and Trinity	38	Slavery, Righteousness
		39	Disease, Truth
		40	Trial, Testing, Tribulation
4	Creation, World	41	Deception
5	Grace, Death	42	Israel's Oppression, 2nd Coming
6	Man's Number, Satan, His Influence	44	Perdition
		45	Preservation, Inheritance
7	Completeness, Spiritual, Perfection	46	Holy Spirit, 2nd Death
		48	Tabernacle, Dwelling Place
8	New Beginning, New Creation, New Birth	49	Wrath of God
		50	Spirit, Holy Ghost, Israel's Jubilee
9	Fruit of the Spirit, Divine Completeness, From the Lord	51	Divine Revelation (51 Books)
10	Testimony, Law and Responsibility	54	Security of the Believer
		60	Pride
11	Judgment and Disorder	65	Apostasy, Abandonment of a Religious Belief
12	Governmental Perfection, Divine Power, Rule or Authority	66	Image or Idol Worship
		70	Israel's Restoration
13	Depravity, Lost and Rebellious	77	Vengeance
14	Deliverance and Salvation	91	Casting Out
15	Rest	99	Seal
16	Love	100	God's Election
17	Victory	105	Calling on the Name of the Lord
18	Bondage	119	Resurrection or Lord's Day
19	Faith	120	Divine Period of Probation
20	Redemption, Expectancy	144	The Spirit Guided Life
21	Exceeding Sinfulness of Sin	153	Fruit Bearing
22	Light, Making Manifest	200	Insufficiency of Earthly/Fleshly Things
23	Death	390	Number of Israel
24	Priesthood	400	Period of Divine Perfection
25	Forgiveness of Sins	430	Promise to the Law, Sojourning
26	Gospel of Christ	490	Spiritual Perfection, (Seventy x Seven), Israel's Complete and Final Restoration
27	Preaching of the Gospel, Prophecy		
28	Eternal Life	600	Warfare
29	Departure	666	Number of Man, Man of Sin, Devil, Satan
30	Dedication or Blood of Christ		
31	Offspring, Seed	888	1st Resurrection of Saints
32	Covenant	1000	Number of the Glory of God, Divine Completion
33	Promise		
34	Naming of a Son, Endurance		
35	Hope		

A collection of scriptures by **Tonya Truster**

NOTES

_____
_____
_____
_____
_____
_____
_____
_____
_____
_____
_____
_____
_____
_____
_____
_____
_____
_____
_____
_____
_____
_____
_____
_____
_____
_____
_____
_____

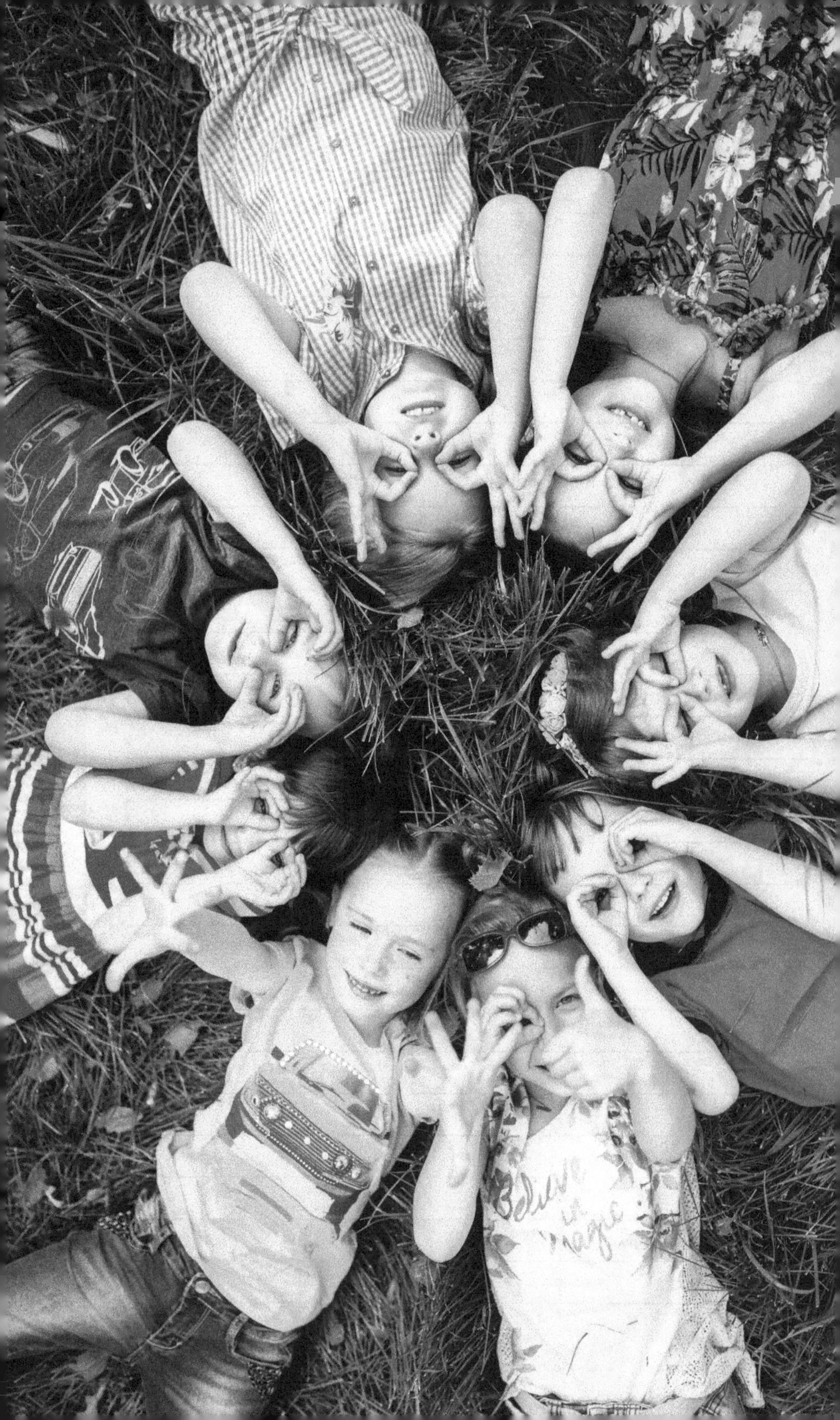
Believe in magic

Children & Discipline

Children are a precious gift, blessing, and legacy bestowed to us by the Lord. Within the pages of sacred scripture, profound guidance is offered to those entrusted with the upbringing of children. These verses from Joshua, Psalms, Proverbs, Titus, and more encapsulate timeless wisdom on the responsibility, blessing, and discipline of raising children in alignment with divine principles. They remind us that discipline, rooted in love and guided by divine example, is essential for the flourishing of the child's soul. From the declaration of devotion in Joshua to the admonitions of discipline in Proverbs, these passages serve as beacons, illuminating the path toward nurturing children in faith, wisdom, and love. As we delve into these teachings, may they empower us to cultivate a generation rooted in the timeless truths of scripture.

I encourage you to pray for God's graceful guidance as you read, meditate on, and memorize the chosen scripture revealed to you by the Holy Spirit.

Children

Joshua 24:15
[15]And if it seem evil unto you to serve the LORD, choose you this day whom ye will serve; whether the gods which your fathers served that [were] on the other side of the flood, or the gods of the Amorites, in whose land ye dwell: but as for me and my house, we will serve the LORD.

Psalm 127:3
[3]Lo, children are an heritage of the LORD: and the fruit of the womb is his reward.

Psalm 139:14
[14]I will praise thee; for I am fearfully and wonderfully made: marvelous are thy works; and that my soul knoweth right well.

Proverbs 22:6
[6]Train up a child in the way he should go: and when he is old, he will not depart from it.

Titus 2:1-8
[1]But speak thou the things which become sound doctrine: [2]That the aged men be sober, grave, temperate, sound in faith, in charity, in patience. [3]The aged women likewise, that they be in behaviour as becometh holiness, not false accusers, not given to much wine, teachers of good things; [4]That they

may teach the young women to be sober, to love their husbands, to love their children, [5]To be discreet, chaste, keepers at home, good, obedient to their own husbands, that the word of God be not blasphemed. [6]Young men likewise exhort to be sober minded. [7]In all things shewing thyself a pattern of good works: in doctrine shewing uncorruptness, gravity, sincerity, [8]Sound speech, that cannot be condemned; that he that is of the contrary part may be ashamed, having no evil thing to say of you.

Discipline

Proverbs 13:24
[24]He that spareth his rod hateth his son: but he that loveth him chasteneth him betimes.

Proverbs 19:18
[18]Chasten thy son while there is hope, and let not thy soul spare for his crying.

Proverbs 22:15
[15]Foolishness is bound in the heart of a child; but the rod of correction shall drive it far from him.

A collection of scriptures by **Tonya Truster**

Proverbs 23:12-14
¹²Apply thine heart unto instruction, and thine ears to the words of knowledge. ¹³Withhold not correction from the child: for if thou beatest him with the rod, he shall not die. ¹⁴Thou shalt beat him with the rod, and shalt deliver his soul from hell.

Proverbs 29:15
¹⁵The rod and reproof give wisdom: but a child left to himself bringeth his mother to shame.

Psalm 89:32
³²Then will I visit their transgression with the rod, and their iniquity with stripes.

2 Samuel 7:14
¹⁴I will be his father, and he shall be my son. If he commit iniquity, I will chasten him with the rod of men, and with the stripes of the children of men.

Proverbs 3:11-12
¹¹My son, despise not the chastening of the LORD; neither be weary of his correction: ¹²For whom the LORD loveth he correcteth; even as a father the son in whom he delighteth.

Hebrews 12:5-11
⁵And ye have forgotten the exhortation which speaketh unto you as unto children, My son, despise not thou the chastening of the Lord, nor faint when thou art rebuked of him: ⁶For whom the Lord loveth he chasteneth, and scourgeth every son whom he receiveth. ⁷If ye endure chastening, God dealeth with you as with sons; for what son is he whom the father chasteneth not? ⁸But if ye be without chastisement, whereof all are partakers, then are ye bastards, and not sons. ⁹Furthermore we have had fathers of our flesh which corrected us, and we gave them reverence: shall we not much rather be in subjection unto the Father of spirits, and live? ¹⁰For they verily for a few days chastened us after their own pleasure; but he for our profit, that we might be partakers of his holiness. ¹¹Now no chastening for the present seemeth to be joyous, but grievous: nevertheless afterward it yieldeth the peaceable fruit of righteousness unto them which are exercised thereby.

CHILDREN MEMORY VERSES:

Ephesians 6:1-2
¹Children, obey your parents in the Lord: for this is right. ²Honour thy father and mother; which is the first commandment with promise.

Colossians 3:20-21
²⁰Children, obey your parents in all things: for this is well pleasing unto the Lord. ²¹Fathers, provoke not your children to anger, lest they be discouraged.

NOTES

_____
_____
_____
_____
_____
_____
_____
_____
_____
_____
_____
_____
_____
_____
_____
_____
_____
_____
_____
_____
_____
_____
_____
_____
_____
_____

Forgiveness & Kindness

In the verses that follow, we embark on a journey through the scriptures, delving into the profound themes of forgiveness and kindness. Rooted in the timeless wisdom of the Old Testament and echoed in the teachings of the New Testament, these passages offer invaluable insights into the transformative power of forgiveness and the boundless depth of divine kindness. As we explore these verses, we are reminded of the grace filled with forgiveness that God extends to us, a mercy so profound that it serves as the ultimate model for our own forgiveness of others. May these scriptures illuminate our hearts and minds, guiding us toward lives filled with grace, compassion, and reconciliation.

I encourage you to pray for God's graceful guidance as you read, meditate on, and memorize the chosen scripture revealed to you by the Holy Spirit.

Forgiveness

Ephesians 4:31-32
[31]Let all bitterness, and wrath, and anger, and clamour, and evil speaking, be put away from you, with all malice: [32]And be ye kind one to another, tenderhearted, forgiving one another, even as God for Christ's sake hath forgiven you.

1 Samuel 16:7
[7]But the LORD said unto Samuel, Look not on his countenance, or on the height of his stature; because I have refused him: for the LORD seeth not as man seeth; for man looketh on the outward appearance, but the LORD looketh on the heart.

Matthew 6:14-15
[14]For if ye forgive men their trespasses, your heavenly Father will also forgive you: [15]But if ye forgive not men their trespasses, neither will your Father forgive your trespasses.

Matthew 18:21-22
[21]Then came Peter to him, and said, Lord, how oft shall my brother sin against me, and I forgive him? till seven times? [22]Jesus saith unto him, I say not unto thee, Until seven times: but, Until seventy times seven.

Luke 6:37
[37]Judge not, and ye shall not be judged: condemn not, and ye shall not be condemned: forgive, and ye shall be forgiven.

Colossians 3:13

[13]Forbearing one another, and forgiving one another, if any man have a quarrel against any: even as Christ forgave you, so also do ye.

KINDNESS

Galatians 5:22-23

[22]But the fruit of the Spirit is love, joy, peace, longsuffering, gentleness, goodness, faith, [23]Meekness, temperance: against such there is no law.

Ephesians 4:31-32

[31]Let all bitterness, and wrath, and anger, and clamour, and evil speaking, be put away from you, with all malice: [32]And be ye kind one to another, tenderhearted, forgiving one another, even as God for Christ's sake hath forgiven you.

Colossians 3:12 & 14

[12]Put on therefore, as the elect of God, holy and beloved, bowels of mercies, kindness, humbleness of mind, meekness, longsuffering; [14]And above all these things put on charity, which is the bond of perfectness.

Titus 3:2-5

[2]To speak evil of no man, to be no brawlers, but gentle, shewing all meekness unto all men. [3]For we ourselves also were sometimes foolish, disobedient, deceived, serving divers lusts and pleasures, living in malice and envy, hateful, and hating one another. [4]But after that the kindness and love of God our Saviour toward man appeared, [5]Not by works of righteousness which we have done, but according to his mercy he saved us, by the washing of regeneration, and renewing of the Holy Ghost;

2 Peter 1:4-9

[4]Whereby are given unto us exceeding great and precious promises: that by these ye might be partakers of the divine nature, having escaped the corruption that is in the world through lust. [5]And beside this, giving all diligence, add to your faith virtue; and to virtue knowledge; [6]And to knowledge temperance; and to temperance patience; and to patience godliness; [7]And to godliness brotherly kindness; and to brotherly kindness charity. [8]For if these things be in you, and abound, they make you that ye shall neither be barren nor unfruitful in the knowledge of our Lord Jesus Christ. [9]But he that lacketh these things is blind, and cannot see afar off, and hath forgotten that he was purged from his old sins.

A collection of scriptures by **Tonya Truster**

Notes

_____
_____
_____
_____
_____
_____
_____
_____
_____
_____
_____
_____
_____
_____
_____
_____
_____
_____
_____
_____
_____
_____
_____
_____
_____
_____
_____
_____
_____
_____

NOTES

*A collection of scriptures by **Tonya Truster***

NOTES

_____
_____
_____
_____
_____
_____
_____
_____
_____
_____
_____
_____
_____
_____
_____
_____
_____
_____
_____
_____
_____
_____
_____
_____
_____
_____

HEART

Within the depths of the human heart lies a vast spectrum of emotions, motivations, and intentions. From the words we speak to the deeds we perform, our hearts are the wellspring of our actions and the core of our being. In the verses that follow, we embark on a journey through the scriptures, exploring the profound significance of the heart and its role in shaping our lives. From the warnings against pride and deceit to the exhortations to humility and trust, these passages offer timeless wisdom and guidance for navigating the complexities of the human heart.

If you seek to understand the heart of God, look no further than Psalm 119, often regarded as the heartbeat of God within the Bible. Positioned at the center of the scriptures, much like the heart is at the center of our bodies, Psalm 119 provides a rich tapestry of devotion, wisdom, and reverence for God's word. As we delve into these verses, may we gain insight into the importance of guarding our hearts, cultivating virtues such as humility and patience, and entrusting ourselves to the transformative power of God's love.

I encourage you to pray for God's graceful guidance as you read, meditate on, and memorize the chosen scripture revealed to you by the Holy Spirit.

Please spend time reading Psalm 119.

Hebrews 4:12
[12]For the word of God is quick, and powerful, and sharper than any twoedged sword, piercing even to the dividing asunder of soul and spirit, and of the joints and marrow, and is a discerner of the thoughts and intents of the heart.

Matthew 12:34-35
[34]O generation of vipers, how can ye, being evil, speak good things? for out of the abundance of the heart the mouth speaketh. [35]A good man out of the good treasure of the heart bringeth forth good things: and an evil man out of the evil treasure bringeth forth evil things.

Joshua 22:5
[5]But take diligent heed to do the commandment and the law, which Moses the servant of the LORD charged you, to love the LORD your God, and to walk in all his ways, and to keep his commandments, and to cleave unto him, and to serve him with all your heart and with all your soul.

Jeremiah 17:9-10

[9]The heart is deceitful above all things, and desperately wicked: who can know it? [10]I the LORD search the heart, I try the reins, even to give every man according to his ways, and according to the fruit of his doings.

Proverbs 3:5-6

[5]Trust in the LORD with all thine heart; and lean not unto thine own understanding. [6]In all thy ways acknowledge him, and he shall direct thy paths.

Proverbs 4:23

[23]Keep thy heart with all diligence; for out of it are the issues of life.

Proverbs 6:16-21

[16]These six things doth the LORD hate: yea, seven are an abomination unto him: [17]A proud look, a lying tongue, and hands that shed innocent blood, [18]An heart that deviseth wicked imaginations, feet that be swift in running to mischief, [19]A false witness that speaketh lies, and he that soweth discord among brethren. [20]My son, keep thy father's commandment, and forsake not the law of thy mother: [21]Bind them continually upon thine heart, and tie them about thy neck.

A collection of scriptures by **Tonya Truster**

Proverbs 15:25

[25]The LORD will destroy the house of the proud: but he will establish the border of the widow.

Proverbs 16:5

[5]Every one that is proud in heart is an abomination to the LORD: though hand join in hand, he shall not be unpunished.

Proverbs 21:4 & 24

[4]An high look, and a proud heart, and the plowing of the wicked, is sin. [24]Proud and haughty scorner is his name, who dealeth in proud wrath.

Proverbs 28:25-26

[25]He that is of a proud heart stirreth up strife: but he that putteth his trust in the LORD shall be made fat. [26]He that trusteth in his own heart is a fool: but whoso walketh wisely, he shall be delivered.

James 4:6-7 & 10

[6]But he giveth more grace. Wherefore he saith, God resisteth the proud, but giveth grace unto the humble. [7]Submit yourselves therefore to God. Resist the devil, and he will flee from you. [10]Humble yourselves in the sight of the Lord, and he shall lift you up.

1 Peter 5:5-8

[5]Likewise, ye younger, submit yourselves unto the elder. Yea, all of you be subject one to another, and be clothed with humility: for God resisteth the proud, and giveth grace to the humble. [6]Humble yourselves therefore under the mighty hand of God, that he may exalt you in due time: [7]Casting all your care upon him; for he careth for you. [8]Be sober, be vigilant; because your adversary the devil, as a roaring lion, walketh about, seeking whom he may devour.

Proverbs 24:1-2

[1]Be not thou envious against evil men, neither desire to be with them. [2]For their heart studieth destruction, and their lips talk of mischief.

Proverbs 23:17

[17]Let not thine heart envy sinners: but be thou in the fear of the LORD all the day long.

Psalm 112:7-8

[7]He shall not be afraid of evil tidings: his heart is fixed, trusting in the LORD. [8]His heart is established, he shall not be afraid, until he see his desire upon his enemies.

Psalm 108:1
[1]O God, my heart is fixed; I will sing and give praise, even with my glory.

Psalm 90:12
[12]So teach us to number our days, that we may apply our hearts unto wisdom.

Psalm 66:18-20
[18]If I regard iniquity in my heart, the Lord will not hear me: [19]But verily God hath heard me; he hath attended to the voice of my prayer. [20]Blessed be God, which hath not turned away my prayer, nor his mercy from me.

Psalm 61:1-2
[1]Hear my cry, O God; attend unto my prayer. [2]From the end of the earth will I cry unto thee, when my heart is overwhelmed: lead me to the rock that is higher than I.

Psalm 57:7
[7]My heart is fixed, O God, my heart is fixed: I will sing and give praise.

Psalm 51:10
[10]Create in me a clean heart, O God; and renew a right spirit within me.

Psalm 40:8
[8]I delight to do thy will, O my God: yea, thy law is within my heart.

Psalm 37:4-5
[4]Delight thyself also in the LORD; and he shall give thee the desires of thine heart. [5]Commit thy way unto the LORD; trust also in him; and he shall bring it to pass.

Psalm 27:14
[14]Wait on the LORD: be of good courage, and he shall strengthen thine heart: wait, I say, on the LORD.

Psalm 19:14
[14]Let the words of my mouth, and the meditation of my heart, be acceptable in thy sight, O LORD, my strength, and my redeemer.

Luke 8:15
[15]But that on the good ground are they, which in an honest and good heart, having heard the word, keep it, and bring forth fruit with patience.

Romans 5:3-5
[3]And not only so, but we glory in tribulations also: knowing that tribulation worketh patience; [4]And patience, experience; and experience, hope: [5]And hope maketh not ashamed; because the love of God is shed abroad in our hearts by the Holy Ghost which is given unto us.

HEART

*A collection of scriptures by **Tonya Truster***

NOTES

_____
_____
_____
_____
_____
_____
_____
_____
_____
_____
_____
_____
_____
_____
_____
_____
_____
_____
_____
_____
_____
_____
_____
_____
_____
_____
_____
_____

HEART

NOTES

NOTES

_____
_____
_____
_____
_____
_____
_____
_____
_____
_____
_____
_____
_____
_____
_____
_____
_____
_____
_____
_____
_____
_____
_____
_____
_____

HEART

MARRIAGE

Marriage, a sacred covenant ordained by God, is a union to be cherished and nurtured. In the following verses, we delve into the timeless wisdom of scripture regarding the sanctity of marriage, the roles of husbands and wives, and the importance of building a strong foundation rooted in faith and love.

However, I recognize that marriages may face trials and tribulations, and sometimes seeking counsel becomes necessary. The Word of God advises us to seek wise and biblically grounded guidance when navigating marital challenges. Therefore, if you find yourself grappling with marital issues, I encourage you to seek biblical marriage counseling from a trusted Christian counselor or pastor within your church community.

Moreover, while divorce is a difficult and often heart-wrenching decision, scripture acknowledges that there can be biblical grounds for divorce. Yet, it is crucial to seek counsel and discernment from a Christian perspective before taking such a significant step.

As we explore these verses, may they serve as a beacon of hope and guidance, leading us to honor God in our marriages and to cultivate relationships built upon love, respect, and mutual submission. Remember, the importance of placing God first, your spouse second, and your family and friends third cannot be overstated. A marriage must have a solid foundation with God as the final authority in your lives as individuals and as a couple.

I encourage you to pray for God's graceful guidance as you read, meditate on, and memorize the chosen scripture revealed to you by the Holy Spirit.

Joshua 24:15
[15]And if it seem evil unto you to serve the LORD, choose you this day whom ye will serve; whether the gods which your fathers served that were on the other side of the flood, or the gods of the Amorites, in whose land ye dwell: **but as for me and my house, we will serve the LORD.**

Proverbs 14:1
[1]Every wise woman buildeth her house: but the foolish plucketh it down with her hands.

Proverbs 24:3-4
[3]Through wisdom is an house builded; and by understanding it is established: [4]And by knowledge shall the chambers be filled with all precious and pleasant riches.

2 Corinthians 6:14
[14]Be ye not unequally yoked together with unbelievers: for what fellowship hath righteousness with unrighteousness? and what communion hath light with darkness?

Titus 2:1-8

[1]But speak thou the things which become sound doctrine: [2]That the aged men be sober, grave, temperate, sound in faith, in charity, in patience. [3]The aged women likewise, that they be in behaviour as becometh holiness, not false accusers, not given to much wine, teachers of good things; [4]That they may teach the young women to be sober, to love their husbands, to love their children, [5]To be discreet, chaste, keepers at home, good, obedient to their own husbands, that the word of God be not blasphemed. [6]Young men likewise exhort to be sober minded. [7]In all things shewing thyself a pattern of good works: in doctrine shewing uncorruptness, gravity, sincerity, [8]Sound speech, that cannot be condemned; that he that is of the contrary part may be ashamed, having no evil thing to say of you.

Ephesians 5:22-33

[22]Wives, submit yourselves unto your own husbands, as unto the Lord. [23]For the husband is the head of the wife, even as Christ is the head of the church: and he is the saviour of the body. [24]Therefore as the church is subject unto Christ, so let the wives be to their own husbands in every thing. [25]Husbands, love your wives, even as Christ also loved the church, and gave himself for it; [26]That he might sanctify and cleanse it with the washing of water by the word, [27]That he might present it to himself a glorious church, not having spot, or wrinkle, or any such thing; but that it should be holy and without blemish. [28]So ought men to love their wives as their own bodies. He that loveth his wife loveth himself. [29]For no man ever yet hated his own flesh; but nourisheth and cherisheth it, even as the Lord the church: [30]For we are members of his body, of his flesh, and of his bones. [31]For this cause shall a man leave his father and mother, and shall be joined unto his wife, and they two shall be one flesh. [32]This is a great mystery: but I speak concerning Christ and the church. [33]Nevertheless let every one of you in particular so love his wife even as himself; and the wife see that she reverence her husband.

Genesis 2:18

[18]And the LORD God said, It is not good that the man should be alone; I will make him an help meet for him.

Matthew 19:5-6

[5]And said, For this cause shall a man leave father and mother, and shall cleave to his wife: and they twain shall be one flesh? [6]Wherefore they are no more twain, but one flesh. What therefore God hath joined together, let not man put asunder.

1 Corinthians 7:8-17

[8]I say therefore to the unmarried and widows, It is good for them if they abide even as I. [9]But if they cannot contain, let them marry: for it is better to marry than to burn. [10]And unto the married I command, yet not I, but the Lord, Let not the

wife depart from her husband: ¹¹But and if she depart, let her remain unmarried, or be reconciled to her husband: and let not the husband put away his wife. ¹²But to the rest speak I, not the Lord: If any brother hath a wife that believeth not, and she be pleased to dwell with him, let him not put her away. ¹³And the woman which hath an husband that believeth not, and if he be pleased to dwell with her, let her not leave him. ¹⁴For the unbelieving husband is sanctified by the wife, and the unbelieving wife is sanctified by the husband: else were your children unclean; but now are they holy. ¹⁵But if the unbelieving depart, let him depart. A brother or a sister is not under bondage in such cases: but God hath called us to peace. ¹⁶For what knowest thou, O wife, whether thou shalt save thy husband? or how knowest thou, O man, whether thou shalt save thy wife? ¹⁷But as God hath distributed to every man, as the Lord hath called every one, so let him walk. And so ordain I in all churches.

Romans 7:2-4
²For the woman which hath an husband is bound by the law to her husband so long as he liveth; but if the husband be dead, she is loosed from the law of her husband. ³So then if, while her husband liveth, she be married to another man, she shall be called an adulteress: but if her husband be dead, she is free from that law; so that she is no adulteress, though she be married to another man. ⁴Wherefore, my brethren, ye also are become dead to the law by the body of Christ; that ye should be married to another, even to him who is raised from the dead, that we should bring forth fruit unto God.

NOTES

*A collection of scriptures by **Tonya Truster***

NOTES

_____
_____
_____
_____
_____
_____
_____
_____
_____
_____
_____
_____
_____
_____
_____
_____
_____
_____
_____
_____
_____
_____
_____
_____
_____
_____

Mourning

In times of grief and sorrow, the comforting embrace of scripture offers solace and hope to weary souls. These verses speak to the tender compassion of God, who walks alongside us in our moments of mourning and despair, offering comfort, healing, and the promise of eternal peace.

Revelation 21:4 paints a picture of a future where pain, sorrow, and death are no more, where God Himself wipes away every tear from our eyes. This vision of restoration and renewal brings reassurance to those who mourn, reminding them that their sorrow will one day be transformed into everlasting joy.

Matthew 5:4 echoes this sentiment, declaring that those who mourn will be comforted. It is a profound reminder that even in our deepest grief, God's comforting presence is near, ready to soothe our troubled hearts and lift us up with His love.

In Psalm 56:8, God tenderly assures us of the significance of our tears, declaring that He collects each one in a bottle. Furthermore, the poignant moment when Jesus wept, as recorded in John 11:35, underscores the depth of His compassion and understanding for our human experience.

In 1 Thessalonians 4:13, we are encouraged not to grieve as those who have no hope, for we have the assurance of resurrection and eternal life through Jesus Christ. This hope sustains us in our times of loss, guiding us through the darkest valleys and leading us into the light of God's eternal promises.

Throughout scripture, we see examples of God's tender care for the brokenhearted. Psalm 34:18 assures us that the Lord is close to the brokenhearted, offering healing and restoration to those who turn to Him in their pain. Psalm 147:3 reminds us that He heals the broken in heart and binds up their wounds, providing comfort and strength in our times of need.

As we journey through seasons of mourning and sorrow, may these verses serve as a beacon of hope, pointing us to the unfailing love and compassion of our Heavenly Father. In His presence, we find solace, peace, and the promise of a brighter tomorrow.

*I encourage you to pray for God's graceful guidance
as you read, meditate on, and memorize the chosen
scripture revealed to you by the Holy Spirit.*

Revelation 21:4

[4]And God shall wipe away all tears from their eyes; and there shall be no more death, neither sorrow, nor crying, neither shall there be any more pain: for the former things are passed away.

Psalm 56:8

[8]Thou tellest my wanderings: put thou my tears into thy bottle: are they not in thy book?

Matthew 5:4

[4]Blessed are they that mourn: for they shall be comforted.

1 Thessalonians 4:13

[13]But I would not have you to be ignorant, brethren, concerning them which are asleep, that ye sorrow not, even as others which have no hope.

John 11:25-26

[25]Jesus said unto her, I am the resurrection, and the life: he that believeth in me, though he were dead, yet shall he live: [26]And whosoever liveth and believeth in me shall never die. Believest thou this?

Isaiah 61:2-3

[2]To proclaim the acceptable year of the LORD, and the day of vengeance of our God; to comfort all that mourn; [3]To appoint unto them that mourn in Zion, to give unto them beauty for ashes, the oil of joy for mourning, the garment of praise for the spirit of heaviness; that they might be called trees of righteousness, the planting of the LORD, that he might be glorified.

Psalm 34:18

[18]The LORD is nigh unto them that are of a broken heart; and saveth such as be of a contrite spirit.

Psalm 116:15

[15]Precious in the sight of the LORD is the death of his saints.

John 11:35

[35]Jesus wept.

Isaiah 41:10

[10]Fear thou not; for I am with thee: be not dismayed; for I am thy God: I will strengthen thee; yea, I will help thee; yea, I will uphold thee with the right hand of my righteousness.

2 Corinthians 1:3-4

[3]Blessed be God, even the Father of our Lord Jesus Christ, the Father of mercies, and the God of all comfort; [4]Who comforteth us in all our tribulation, that we may be able to comfort them which are in any trouble, by the comfort wherewith we ourselves are comforted of God.

Psalm 30:5

[5]For his anger endureth but a moment; in his favour is life: weeping may endure for a night, but joy cometh in the morning.

Romans 10:9

[9]That if thou shalt confess with thy mouth the Lord Jesus, and shalt believe in thine heart that God hath raised him from the dead, thou shalt be saved.

Ecclesiastes 7:4

[4]The heart of the wise is in the house of mourning; but the heart of fools is in the house of mirth.

1 Thessalonians 4:13-14

[13]But I would not have you to be ignorant, brethren, concerning them which are asleep, that ye sorrow not, even as others which have no hope. [14]For if we believe that Jesus died and rose again, even so them also which sleep in Jesus will God bring with him.

Matthew 2:18

[18]In Rama was there a voice heard, lamentation, and weeping, and great mourning, Rachel weeping for her children, and would not be comforted, because they are not.

1 Samuel 30:4

[4]Then David and the people that were with him lifted up their voice and wept, until they had no more power to weep.

Ezekiel 24:17

[17]Forbear to cry, make no mourning for the dead, bind the tire of thine head upon thee, and put on thy shoes upon thy feet, and cover not thy lips, and eat not the bread of men.

Leviticus 19:28

[28]Ye shall not make any cuttings in your flesh for the dead, nor print any marks upon you: I am the LORD.

2 Corinthians 1:3-5

[3]Blessed be God, even the Father of our Lord Jesus Christ, the Father of mercies, and the God of all comfort; [4]Who comforteth us in all our tribulation, that we may be able to comfort them which are in any trouble, by the comfort wherewith we ourselves are comforted of God. [5]For as the sufferings of Christ abound in us, so our consolation also aboundeth by Christ.

Numbers 20:29

[29]And when all the congregation saw that Aaron was dead, they mourned for Aaron thirty days, even all the house of Israel.

2 Samuel 1:12

[12]And they mourned, and wept, and fasted until even, for Saul, and for Jonathan his son, and for the people of the LORD, and for the house of Israel; because they were fallen by the sword.

Psalm 147:3

[3]He healeth the broken in heart, and bindeth up their wounds.

Genesis 23:2

[2]And Sarah died in Kirjath-arba; the same is Hebron in the land of Canaan: and Abraham came to mourn for Sarah, and to weep for her.

Romans 8:18

[18]For I reckon that the sufferings of this present time are not worthy to be compared with the glory which shall be revealed in us.

Psalm 73:26

[26]My flesh and my heart faileth: but God is the strength of my heart, and my portion for ever.

A collection of scriptures by **Tonya Truster**

Notes

MOURNING

NOTES

NOTES

_____
_____
_____
_____
_____
_____
_____
_____
_____
_____
_____
_____
_____
_____
_____
_____
_____
_____
_____
_____
_____
_____
_____
_____
_____
_____
_____
_____
_____

MOUTH & TONGUE & LIPS

The power of words is a recurring theme throughout the scriptures, underscoring the importance of speech in our lives. In Matthew 12:34-37, Jesus highlights the connection between the heart and the mouth, emphasizing that our words reveal the condition of our hearts and that we will be held accountable for every word spoken. Romans 15:6 encourages believers to unite in glorifying God with one mind and one mouth. Throughout the Psalms, we find expressions of the psalmists' commitment to guard their tongues, offer praise, and seek wisdom in their speech. Proverbs provides numerous insights into the impact of words, urging us to speak with wisdom, kindness, and restraint. From Ecclesiastes to Exodus, the scriptures underscore the significance of our words, reminding us of the weight they carry and the importance of aligning our speech with righteousness and truth. Ultimately, as Romans 10:9-10 declares, confession with our mouths is integral to our salvation, highlighting the profound connection between our words and our faith.

I encourage you to pray for God's graceful guidance as you read, meditate on, and memorize the chosen scripture revealed to you by the Holy Spirit.

Hebrews 4:12
¹²For the word of God is quick, and powerful, and sharper than any twoedged sword, piercing even to the dividing asunder of soul and spirit, and of the joints and marrow, and is a discerner of the thoughts and intents of the heart.

Matthew 12:34-37
³⁴O generation of vipers, how can ye, being evil, speak good things? for out of the abundance of the heart the mouth speaketh. ³⁵A good man out of the good treasure of the heart bringeth forth good things: and an evil man out of the evil treasure bringeth forth evil things. ³⁶But I say unto you, That every idle word that men shall speak, they shall give account thereof in the day of judgment. ³⁷For by thy words thou shalt be justified, and by thy words thou shalt be condemned.

Romans 15:6
⁶That ye may with one mind and one mouth glorify God, even the Father of our Lord Jesus Christ.

Psalm 19:14
¹⁴Let the words of my mouth, and the meditation of my heart, be acceptable in thy sight, O LORD, my strength, and my redeemer.

Psalm 39:1
[1]I said, I will take heed to my ways, that I sin not with my tongue: I will keep my mouth with a bridle, while the wicked is before me.

Psalm 40:3
[3]And he hath put a new song in my mouth, even praise unto our God: many shall see it, and fear, and shall trust in the LORD.

Psalm 63:5
[5]My soul shall be satisfied as with marrow and fatness; and my mouth shall praise thee with joyful lips:

Psalm 71:8 & 15
[8]Let my mouth be filled with thy praise and with thy honour all the day. [15]My mouth shall shew forth thy righteousness and thy salvation all the day; for I know not the numbers thereof.

Psalm 89:1
[1]I will sing of the mercies of the LORD for ever: with my mouth will I make known thy faithfulness to all generations.

Psalm 109:30
[30]I will greatly praise the LORD with my mouth; yea, I will praise him among the multitude.

Psalm 119:103
[103]How sweet are thy words unto my taste! yea, sweeter than honey to my mouth!

Psalm 145:21
[21]My mouth shall speak the praise of the LORD: and let all flesh bless his holy name for ever and ever.

Psalm 141:3
[3]Set a watch, O LORD, before my mouth; keep the door of my lips.

Proverbs 29:11
[11]A fool uttereth all his mind: but a wise man keepeth it in till afterwards.

Proverbs 4:24
[24]Put away from thee a froward mouth, and perverse lips put far from thee.

Proverbs 16:23
[23]The heart of the wise teacheth his mouth, and addeth learning to his lips.

Proverbs 8:13

[13]The fear of the LORD is to hate evil: pride, and arrogancy, and the evil way, and the froward mouth, do I hate.

Proverbs 18:4

[4]The words of a man's mouth are as deep waters, and the wellspring of wisdom as a flowing brook.

Proverbs 31:26

[26]She openeth her mouth with wisdom; and in her tongue is the law of kindness.

Proverbs 13:3

[3]He that keepeth his mouth keepeth his life: but he that openeth wide his lips shall have destruction.

Proverbs 21:23

[23]Whoso keepeth his mouth and his tongue keepeth his soul from troubles.

Proverbs 15:1-4

[1]A soft answer turneth away wrath: but grievous words stir up anger. [2]The tongue of the wise useth knowledge aright: but the mouth of fools poureth out foolishness. [3]The eyes of the Lord are in every place, beholding the evil and the good. [4]A wholesome tongue is a tree of life: but perverseness therein is a breach in the spirit.

Proverbs 11:9

[9]An hypocrite with his mouth destroyeth his neighbour: but through knowledge shall the just be delivered.

Proverbs 26:28

[28]A lying tongue hateth those that are afflicted by it; and a flattering mouth worketh ruin.

Proverbs 10:11

[11]The mouth of a righteous man is a well of life: but violence covereth the mouth of the wicked.

Proverbs 12:6 & 14

[6]The words of the wicked are to lie in wait for blood: but the mouth of the upright shall deliver them. [14]A man shall be satisfied with good by the fruit of his mouth: and the recompence of a man's hands shall be rendered unto him.

Ecclesiastes 10:12
¹²The words of a wise man's mouth are gracious; but the lips of a fool will swallow up himself.

Ecclesiastes 5:2 & 6
²Be not rash with thy mouth, and let not thine heart be hasty to utter any thing before God: for God is in heaven, and thou upon earth: therefore let thy words be few. ⁶Suffer not thy mouth to cause thy flesh to sin; neither say thou before the angel, that it was an error: wherefore should God be angry at thy voice, and destroy the work of thine hands?

Ecclesiastes 6:7
⁷All the labour of man is for his mouth, and yet the appetite is not filled.

Exodus 4:12
¹²Now therefore go, and I will be with thy mouth, and teach thee what thou shalt say.

Exodus 13:9
⁹And it shall be for a sign unto thee upon thine hand, and for a memorial between thine eyes, that the LORD's law may be in thy mouth: for with a strong hand hath the LORD brought thee out of Egypt.

Numbers 30:2-5
²If a man vow a vow unto the LORD, or swear an oath to bind his soul with a bond; he shall not break his word, he shall do according to all that proceedeth out of his mouth. ³If a woman also vow a vow unto the LORD, and bind herself by a bond, being in her father's house in her youth; ⁴And her father hear her vow, and her bond wherewith she hath bound her soul, and her father shall hold his peace at her: then all her vows shall stand, and every bond wherewith she hath bound her soul shall stand. ⁵But if her father disallow her in the day that he heareth; not any of her vows, or of her bonds wherewith she hath bound her soul, shall stand: and the LORD shall forgive her, because her father disallowed her.

Romans 10:9-10
⁹That if thou shalt confess with thy mouth the Lord Jesus, and shalt believe in thine heart that God hath raised him from the dead, thou shalt be saved. ¹⁰For with the heart man believeth unto righteousness; and with the mouth confession is made unto salvation.

NOTES

_____
_____
_____
_____
_____
_____
_____
_____
_____
_____
_____
_____
_____
_____
_____
_____
_____
_____
_____
_____
_____
_____
_____
_____
_____

NOTES

A collection of scriptures by *Tonya Truster*

NOTES

_____
_____
_____
_____
_____
_____
_____
_____
_____
_____
_____
_____
_____
_____
_____
_____
_____
_____
_____
_____
_____
_____
_____
_____
_____
_____
_____

MOUTH & TONGUE & LIPS

I Am
Shalom
Jehovah Shammah
Lion of Judah
The Redeemer
Son of the Most High
Jehovah Nissi
Son of David
Man of Sorrows
The Rock of Ages
EL SHADDAI
Bridegroom
King of the Jews
Rose of Sharon
Emanuel
Bright Morning Star
Mighty One
Shekhinah
YAHWEH
The Angel of the Lord
Deliverer
Elohim
God with us
Jehovah Rapha
Bridegroom
Living Stone
Adonai
The Almighty
Lamb of God
Creator
Bread of Life
Son of Man
Shaddai
True Vine
Jesus Christ
The Way The Truth And The Life
The Good Shepherd
Living God
Deliverer
Cornerstone
Lord Almighty
Advocate
Root of David
Author of Life
Jehovah Jireh
Lamb of God
The Messiah
Lord of Glory
Abba Father
The Living Water
Alpha and Omega
Word of God
Living Stone

NAMES FOR GOD

Name for God	Significance of the Name	Limited Scriptural References for the Name
Abba	Father	Romans 8:15, Mark 14:36, & Galatians 4:1-7
Adonai	Lord - Lord & master - dealing with the Gentiles	Genesis 16:2 & Judges 6:15
Alpha & Omega	beginning & end	Revelation 22:13, 1:8, 21:6-7, 1:17-18, Isaiah 44:6, & 48:12
Christos	anointed one	Many verses about the anointed one - see gospels
El Deah	God of knowledge	Nahum 1:7 & Roman 11:34
El Elyon	God most high	Genesis 14:18-24 & Deuteronomy 26:19
El Eloah	God - mighty, power, strong, & prominent	Nehemiah 9:17, Psalm 139:19, & Gensis 31:29
El Gibhor	mighty God - rule with a rod of iron	Isaiah 9:6
El Olam	everlasting God - without beginning or end	Genesis 21:22-34, Psalm 5:11, & Psalm 90:1-3
El Qanna	LORD is a jealous God	Exodus 20:5, 34:14, Deuteronomy 4:24, 5:9, & 6:15
El Roi	God who sees	Genesis 16:13 & Luke 12:7
El Shaddai	God almighty - mighty one of Jacob	Genesis 49:24 & Psalm 132:2 & 5
Elohim	God - creator, mighty, & strong	Genesis 17:7 & Jeremiah 31:33
Immanuel & Emmanuel	God with us	Isaiah 7:14, Matthew 1:22-23, Numbers 14:9, & Haggai 2:4
Yahweh (YHWH) or Jehovah	I Am - LORD (all caps) - Jehovah LORD - dealing with His people - present, accessible, near, deliverance, forgiveness, & guidance - dealing with the Jews	Exodus 3:13-15, Deuteronomy 6:4, Daniel 9:14, & Psalm 83:18
Yahweh Bore	LORD Creator	Genesis 1:3
Yahweh Elohim	Lord-God Jehovah - the Lord of Lords	Genesis 2:4 & Psalm 59:5
Yahweh Jireh	LORD Jehovah that provides	Genesis 22:14
Yahweh M'Kaddesh	LORD Jehovah that sanctifies, makes holy	Leviticus 20:8
Yahweh Nissi	LORD Jehovah my banner - the rally place - celebrate the victory	Exodus 17:15
Yahweh Rapha	LORD Jehovah that heals	Exodus 15:26
Yahweh Rohi	LORD Jehovah my shepherd	Psalm 23:1
Yahweh Sabaoth/ Tsabbaoth	LORD Jehovah of hosts	Isaiah 1:24 & Psalm 46:7
Yahweh Shalom	LORD Jehovah my peace	Judges 6:24
Yahweh Shammah	LORD Jehovah is always there - with me	Ezekiel 48:35
Yahweh Tsidkenu	LORD Jehovah my righteousness	Jeremiah 33:16

NOTES

NOTES

NAMES FOR GOD

PATIENCE

In the tapestry of life, patience is the golden thread that weaves through the fabric of our experiences, binding together moments of trial and triumph with the steady hand of endurance. From the gentle exhortations of Luke to the resounding declarations of Revelation, the scriptures resound with the call to cultivate patience as we navigate the complexities of existence. As we journey through the verses that exalt patience, let us heed the wisdom they impart, embracing this virtue not only as a hallmark of character but as a guiding light on the path toward spiritual growth and fulfillment. Join in as we delve into the timeless truths of patience, discovering its power to fortify our souls and illuminate our way forward in faith.

I encourage you to pray for God's graceful guidance as you read, meditate on, and memorize the chosen scripture revealed to you by the Holy Spirit.

Luke 8:15
[15]But that on the good ground are they, which in an honest and good heart, having heard the word, keep it, and bring forth fruit with patience.

Luke 21:19
[19]In your patience possess ye your souls.

Romans 5:3-5
[3]And not only so, but we glory in tribulations also: knowing that tribulation worketh patience; [4]And patience, experience; and experience, hope: [5]And hope maketh not ashamed; because the love of God is shed abroad in our hearts by the Holy Ghost which is given unto us.

Romans 8:25
[25]But if we hope for that we see not, then do we with patience wait for it.

Romans 15:4-5
[4]For whatsoever things were written aforetime were written for our learning, that we through patience and comfort of the scriptures might have hope. [5]Now the God of patience and consolation grant you to be likeminded one toward another according to Christ Jesus.

Philippians 4:11
[11]Not that I speak in respect of want: for I have learned, in whatsoever state I am, therewith to be content.

2 Corinthians 6:4-10

[4]But in all things approving ourselves as the ministers of God, in much patience, in afflictions, in necessities, in distresses, [5]In stripes, in imprisonments, in tumults, in labours, in watchings, in fastings; [6]By pureness, by knowledge, by longsuffering, by kindness, by the Holy Ghost, by love unfeigned, [7]By the word of truth, by the power of God, by the armour of righteousness on the right hand and on the left, [8]By honour and dishonour, by evil report and good report: as deceivers, and yet true; [9]As unknown, and yet well known; as dying, and, behold, we live; as chastened, and not killed; [10]As sorrowful, yet alway rejoicing; as poor, yet making many rich; as having nothing, and yet possessing all things.

PATIENCE

*A collection of scriptures by **Tonya Truster***

Colossians 1:11-12

[11]Strengthened with all might, according to his glorious power, unto all patience and longsuffering with joyfulness; [12]Giving thanks unto the Father, which hath made us meet to be partakers of the inheritance of the saints in light.

1 Thessalonians 1:3-4

[3]Remembering without ceasing your work of faith, and labour of love, and patience of hope in our Lord Jesus Christ, in the sight of God and our Father; [4]Knowing, brethren beloved, your election of God.

2 Thessalonians 1:4

[4]So that we ourselves glory in you in the churches of God for your patience and faith in all your persecutions and tribulations that ye endure.

1 Timothy 6:10-11

[10]For the love of money is the root of all evil: which while some coveted after, they have erred from the faith, and pierced themselves through with many sorrows. [11]But thou, O man of God, flee these things; and follow after righteousness, godliness, faith, love, patience, meekness.

2 Timothy 3:10-11

[10]But thou hast fully known my doctrine, manner of life, purpose, faith, longsuffering, charity, patience, [11]Persecutions, afflictions, which came unto me at Antioch, at Iconium, at Lystra; what persecutions I endured: but out of them all the Lord delivered me.

Titus 2:1-8

[1]But speak thou the things which become sound doctrine: [2]That the aged men be sober, grave, temperate, sound in faith, in charity, in patience. [3]The aged women likewise, that they be in behaviour as becometh holiness, not false accusers, not given to much wine, teachers of good things; [4]That they may teach the young women to be sober, to love their husbands, to love their children, [5]To be discreet, chaste, keepers at home, good, obedient to their own husbands, that the word of God be not blasphemed. [6]Young men likewise exhort to be sober minded. [7]In all things shewing thyself a pattern of good works: in doctrine shewing uncorruptness, gravity, sincerity, [8]Sound speech, that cannot be condemned; that he that is of the contrary part may be ashamed, having no evil thing to say of you.

Hebrews 6:12

[12]That ye be not slothful, but followers of them who through faith and patience inherit the promises.

Hebrews 10:36

[36]For ye have need of patience, that, after ye have done the will of God, ye might receive the promise.

Hebrews 12:1-2

[1]Wherefore seeing we also are compassed about with so great a cloud of witnesses, let us lay aside every weight, and the sin which doth so easily beset us, and let us run with patience the race that is set before us, [2]Looking unto Jesus the author and finisher of our faith; who for the joy that was set before him endured the cross, despising the shame, and is set down at the right hand of the throne of God.

James 1:3-4

[3]Knowing this, that the trying of your faith worketh patience. [4]But let patience have her perfect work, that ye may be perfect and entire, wanting nothing.

James 5:7-11

[7]Be patient therefore, brethren, unto the coming of the Lord. Behold, the husbandman waiteth for the precious fruit of the earth, and hath long patience for it, until he receive the early and latter rain. [8]Be ye also patient; stablish your hearts: for the coming of the Lord draweth nigh. [9]Grudge not one against another, brethren, lest ye be condemned: behold, the judge standeth before the door. [10]Take, my brethren, the prophets, who have spoken in the name of the Lord, for an example of suffering affliction, and of patience. [11]Behold, we count them happy which endure. Ye have heard of the patience of Job, and have seen the end of the Lord; that the Lord is very pitiful, and of tender mercy.

2 Peter 1:4-7

[4]Whereby are given unto us exceeding great and precious promises: that by these ye might be partakers of the divine nature, having escaped the corruption that is in the world through lust. [5]And beside this, giving all diligence, add to your faith virtue; and to virtue knowledge; [6]And to knowledge temperance; and to temperance patience; and to patience godliness; [7]And to godliness brotherly kindness; and to brotherly kindness charity.

Revelation 2:1-4

[1]Unto the angel of the church of Ephesus write; These things saith he that holdeth the seven stars in his right hand, who walketh in the midst of the seven golden candlesticks; [2]I know thy works, and thy labour, and thy patience, and how thou canst not bear them which are evil: and thou hast tried them which say they are apostles, and are not, and hast found them liars: [3]And hast borne, and hast patience, and for my name's sake hast laboured, and hast not fainted. [4]Nevertheless I have somewhat against thee, because thou hast left thy first love.

Revelation 3:10

[10]Because thou hast kept the word of my patience, I also will keep thee from the hour of temptation, which shall come upon all the world, to try them that dwell upon the earth.

A collection of scriptures by **Tonya Truster**

NOTES

_____
_____
_____
_____
_____
_____
_____
_____
_____
_____
_____
_____
_____
_____
_____
_____
_____
_____
_____
_____
_____
_____
_____
_____
_____

PATIENCE

NOTES

NOTES

_____

_____

_____

_____

_____

_____

_____

_____

_____

_____

_____

_____

_____

_____

_____

_____

_____

_____

_____

_____

_____

_____

_____

_____

_____

PATIENCE

PEACE

These verses offer profound insights into the peace, strength, and hope that believers find in God. From Jeremiah's assurance of God's plans for our welfare to Paul's exhortation to live peaceably with others, each passage reinforces the comforting truth of God's sovereignty and provision. As we meditate on these promises and submit our desires to Him in prayer, we are reminded of God's faithfulness, His ability to accomplish the impossible, and His steadfast goodness. May these verses inspire you to trust in God's promises, seek His peace, and find strength in His presence, even in the midst of life's challenges.

We frequently encounter the acronym RIP (Rest in Peace) upon someone's passing, yet the wisdom of God's Word extends this notion beyond death. It encourages us to RIP (Rest in Peace) while we are still living. Rest in Peace, assured that God is in control, His timing is perfect, and He holds us securely in His right hand.

I encourage you to pray for God's graceful guidance as you read, meditate on, and memorize the chosen scripture revealed to you by the Holy Spirit.

Jeremiah 29:11
11For I know the thoughts that I think toward you, saith the LORD, thoughts of peace, and not of evil, to give you an expected end.

Jeremiah 32:27
27Behold, I am the LORD, the God of all flesh: is there any thing too hard for me?

Psalm 119:165
165Great peace have they which love thy law: and nothing shall offend them.

Psalm 46:1
1God is my refuge and strength, a very present help in trouble.

Psalm 46:10
10Be still, and know that I am God: I will be exalted among the heathen. I will be exalted in the earth.

Romans 12:18-21
18If it be possible, as much as lieth in you, live peaceably with all men. 19Dearly beloved, avenge not yourselves, but rather give place unto wrath: for it is written, Vengeance is mine; I will repay, saith the Lord. 20Therefore if thine enemy hunger, feed him; if he thirst, give him drink: for in so doing thou shalt heap coals of fire on his head. 21Be not overcome of evil, but overcome evil with good.

Romans 5:1
[1]Therefore being justified by faith, we have peace with God through our Lord Jesus Christ.

Romans 15:13
[13]Now the God of hope fill you with all joy and peace in believing, that ye may abound in hope, through the power of the Holy Ghost.

Isaiah 26:3
[3]Thou wilt keep him in perfect peace, whose mind is stayed on thee: because he trusteth in thee.

Colossians 3:15
[15]And let the peace of God rule in your hearts, to the which also ye are called in one body; and be ye thankful.

Philippians 4:6-7
[6]Be careful for nothing; but in every thing by prayer and supplication with thanksgiving let your requests be made known unto God. [7]And the peace of God, which passeth all understanding, shall keep your hearts and minds through Christ Jesus.

A collection of scriptures by **Tonya Truster**

Philippians 4:11 & 13

[11]Not that I speak in respect of want: for I have learned, in whatsoever state I am, therewith to be content. [13]I can do all things through Christ which strengtheneth me.

Matthew 7:7-8 & 11

[7]Ask, and it shall be given you; seek, and ye shall find; knock, and it shall be opened unto you: [8]For every one that asketh receiveth; and he that seeketh findeth; and to him that knocketh it shall be opened. [11]If ye then, being evil, know how to give good gifts unto your children, how much more shall your Father which is in heaven give good things to them that ask him?

Luke 1:37

[37]For with God nothing shall be impossible.

Mark 11:24

[24]Therefore I say unto you, What things soever ye desire, when ye pray, believe that ye receive them, and ye shall have them.

James 1:17

[17]Every good gift and every perfect gift is from above, and cometh down from the Father of lights, with whom is no variableness, neither shadow of turning.

Isaiah 40:31

[31]But they that wait upon the LORD shall renew their strength; they shall mount up with wings as eagles; they shall run, and not be weary; and they shall walk, and not faint.

1 Corinthians 14:33

[33]For God is not the author of confusion, but of peace, as in all churches of the saints.

2 Corinthians 12:7-10

[7]And lest I should be exalted above measure through the abundance of the revelations, there was given to me a thorn in the flesh, the messenger of Satan to buffet me, lest I should be exalted above measure. [8]For this thing I besought the Lord thrice, that it might depart from me. [9]And he said unto me, My grace is sufficient for thee: for my strength is made perfect in weakness. Most gladly therefore will I rather glory in my infirmities, that the power of Christ may rest upon me. [10]Therefore I take pleasure in infirmities, in reproaches, in necessities, in persecutions, in distresses for Christ's sake: for when I am weak, then am I strong.

NOTES

NOTES

PEACE

RELATIONSHIPS

These verses speak to the importance of relationships and the qualities that make them meaningful and enduring. They emphasize the value of integrity, kindness, humility, and forgiveness in our interactions with others. From choosing a good name over riches to bearing one another's burdens, the passages underscore the significance of mutual support, guidance, and camaraderie. Furthermore, they highlight the wisdom of surrounding ourselves with trustworthy companions and the responsibility we have to be a true friend in return. In essence, they provide a blueprint for fostering healthy, supportive, and enriching relationships that reflect the love and grace of God. Additionally, they emphasize the importance of having our hearts knitted together and being like-minded, promoting unity, understanding, and empathy among individuals.

I encourage you to pray for God's graceful guidance as you read, meditate on, and memorize the chosen scripture revealed to you by the Holy Spirit.

Proverbs 22:1
¹A good name is rather to be chosen than great riches, and loving favour rather than silver and gold.

Colossians 2:2
²That their hearts might be comforted, being knit together in love, and unto all riches of the full assurance of understanding, to the acknowledgement of the mystery of God, and of the Father, and of Christ;

Psalm 112:5
⁵A good man sheweth favour, and lendeth: he will guide his affairs with discretion.

Ecclesiastes 4:9-10
⁹Two are better than one; because they have a good reward for their labour. ¹⁰For if they fall, the one will lift up his fellow: but woe to him that is alone when he falleth; for he hath not another to help him up.

Ephesians 4:32
³²And be ye kind one to another, tenderhearted, forgiving one another, even as God for Christ's sake hath forgiven you.

Galatians 6:2
²Bear ye one another's burdens, and so fulfil the law of Christ.

Proverbs 6:3
[3]Do this now, my son, and deliver thyself, when thou art come into the hand of thy friend; go, humble thyself, and make sure thy friend.

Proverbs 16:19-20
[19]Better it is to be of an humble spirit with the lowly, than to divide the spoil with the proud. [20]He that handleth a matter wisely shall find good: and whoso trusteth in the LORD, happy is he.

Ephesians 4:2-3
[2]With all lowliness and meekness, with longsuffering, forbearing one another in love; [3]Endeavouring to keep the unity of the Spirit in the bond of peace.

Romans 12:18-21
[18]If it be possible, as much as lieth in you, live peaceably with all men. [19]Dearly beloved, avenge not yourselves, but rather give place unto wrath: for it is written, Vengeance is mine; I will repay, saith the Lord. [20]Therefore if thine enemy hunger, feed him; if he thirst, give him drink: for in so doing thou shalt heap coals of fire on his head. [21]Be not overcome of evil, but overcome evil with good.

Philippians 2:2-4
[2]Fulfil ye my joy, that ye be likeminded, having the same love, being of one accord, of one mind. [3]Let nothing be done through strife or vainglory; but in lowliness of mind let each esteem other better than themselves. [4]Look not every man on his own things, but every man also on the things of others.

1 Thessalonians 5:11
[11]Wherefore comfort yourselves together, and edify one another, even as also ye do.

Proverbs 24:1-2
[1]Be not thou envious against evil men, neither desire to be with them. [2]For their heart studieth destruction, and their lips talk of mischief.

Proverbs 18:24
[24]A man that hath friends must shew himself friendly: and there is a friend that sticketh closer than a brother.

A collection of scriptures by **Tonya Truster**

Notes

_____

_____

_____

_____

_____

_____

_____

_____

_____

_____

_____

_____

_____

_____

_____

_____

_____

_____

_____

_____

_____

_____

_____

_____

NOTES

NOTES

_____
_____
_____
_____
_____
_____
_____
_____
_____
_____
_____
_____
_____
_____
_____
_____
_____
_____
_____
_____
_____
_____
_____
_____
_____
_____
_____
_____
_____
_____
_____
_____

SALVATION & ETERNAL SECURITY & BAPTISM

These verses delve into three fundamental aspects of Christian faith: Salvation, Eternal Security, and Baptism.

First, Salvation is depicted as a free gift from God, attained through faith in Jesus Christ. The passages affirm the universality of sin and the divine intervention through Christ's sacrifice on the cross, offering eternal life to those who believe.

Second, Eternal Security assures believers of the unbreakable bond they have with God through Christ. They testify to the unyielding love of God and the assurance of eternal life in heaven with God for those who have accepted Jesus as their Savior.

Lastly, Baptism symbolizes spiritual rebirth and signifies union with Christ in His death, burial, and resurrection. The verses underscore the transformative nature of baptism, marking the beginning of a new life dedicated to righteousness and service to God.

Together, these passages encapsulate the core tenets of Christian faith, highlighting God's grace, the security of believers in His love, and the significance of baptism as a public declaration of one's commitment to Christ.

I encourage you to pray for God's graceful guidance as you read, meditate on, and memorize the chosen scripture revealed to you by the Holy Spirit.

SALVATION

John 3:16
[16]For God so loved the world, that he gave his only begotten Son, that whosoever believeth in him should not perish, but have everlasting life.

Romans 3:10
[10]As it is written, There is none righteous, no, not one.

Romans 3:22-23
[22]Even the righteousness of God which is by faith of Jesus Christ unto all and upon all them that believe: for there is no difference. [23]For all have sinned, and come short of the glory of God.

Romans 5:8 & 12

[8]But God commendeth his love toward us, in that, while we were yet sinners, Christ died for us. [12]Wherefore, as by one man sin entered into the world, and death by sin; and so death passed upon all men, for that all have sinned.

Romans 6:23

[23]For the wages of sin is death; but the gift of God is eternal life through Jesus Christ our Lord.

Ephesians 2:8-9

[8]For by grace are ye saved through faith; and that not of yourselves: it is the gift of God: [9]Not of works, lest any man should boast.

Romans 10:9-10, 13

[9]That if thou shalt confess with thy mouth the Lord Jesus, and shalt believe in thine heart that God hath raised him from the dead, thou shalt be saved. [10]For with the heart man believeth unto righteousness; and with the mouth confession is made unto salvation. [13]For whosoever shall call upon the name of the Lord shall be saved.

ETERNAL SECURITY

1 John 5:12-13

[12]He that hath the Son hath life; and he that hath not the Son of God hath not life. [13]These things have I written unto you that believe on the name of the Son of God; that ye may know that ye have eternal life, and that ye may believe on the name of the Son of God.

Romans 8:35-39

[35]Who shall separate us from the love of Christ? shall tribulation, or distress, or persecution, or famine, or nakedness, or peril, or sword? [36]As it is written, For thy sake we are killed all the day long; we are accounted as sheep for the slaughter. [37]Nay, in all these things we are more than conquerors through him that loved us. [38]For I am persuaded, that neither death, nor life, nor angels, nor principalities, nor powers, nor things present, nor things to come, [39]Nor height, nor depth, nor any other creature, shall be able to separate us from the love of God, which is in Christ Jesus our Lord.

Ephesians 1:12-14

[12]That we should be to the praise of his glory, who first trusted in Christ. [13]In whom ye also trusted, after that ye heard the word of truth, the gospel of your salvation: in whom also after that ye believed, ye were sealed with that holy Spirit of promise, [14]Which is the earnest of our inheritance until the redemption of the purchased possession, unto the praise of his glory.

A collection of scriptures by **Tonya Truster**

1 Corinthians 12:12-13

[12]For as the body is one, and hath many members, and all the members of that one body, being many, are one body: so also is Christ. [13]For by one Spirit are we all baptized into one body, whether we be Jews or Gentiles, whether we be bond or free; and have been all made to drink into one Spirit.

Romans 6:1-7

[1]What shall we say then? Shall we continue in sin, that grace may abound? [2]God forbid. How shall we, that are dead to sin, live any longer therein? [3]Know ye not, that so many of us as were baptized into Jesus Christ were baptized into his death? [4]Therefore we are buried with him by baptism into death: that like as Christ was raised up from the dead by the glory of the Father, even so we also should walk in newness of life. [5]For if we have been planted together in the likeness of his death, we shall be also in the likeness of his resurrection: [6]Knowing this, that our old man is crucified with him, that the body of sin might be destroyed, that henceforth we should not serve sin. [7]For he that is dead is freed from sin.

Matthew 3:13-17

[13]Then cometh Jesus from Galilee to Jordan unto John, to be baptized of him. [14]But John forbad him, saying, I have need to be baptized of thee, and comest thou to me? [15]And Jesus answering said unto him, Suffer it to be so now: for thus it becometh us to fulfil all righteousness. Then he suffered him. [16]And Jesus, when he was baptized, went up straightway out of the water: and, lo, the heavens were opened unto him, and he saw the Spirit of God descending like a dove, and lighting upon him: [17]And lo a voice from heaven, saying, This is my beloved Son, in whom I am well pleased.

NOTES

NOTES

SATAN/DEVIL/LUCIFER FALLS FROM HEAVEN

Within the tapestry of biblical narratives, the figure of Satan, also known as the Devil or Lucifer, emerges as a central antagonist in the cosmic drama between good and evil. From Genesis, the beginning of humanity's existence, in the Garden of Eden to the apocalyptic visions of Revelation, scriptures provide insights into the nature, tactics, and ultimate fate of this malevolent entity.

Genesis lays the groundwork, revealing Satan's deceptive influence in tempting Eve. Job offers a glimpse into the celestial court, where Satan challenges the faithfulness of God's servants. Throughout the Old and New Testaments, references abound to Satan's schemes, lies, and attempts to thwart the divine plan.

In the New Testament, Satan's encounters with Jesus underscore the ongoing spiritual warfare, as Christ rebuffs temptation and exposes the adversary's strategies. From manipulating minds to inflicting suffering, Satan's presence looms large, yet scriptures also proclaim the triumph of God's sovereignty over darkness.

Amidst the grand narrative, however, lies a cautionary tale for believers: Satan's subtle ways of deception. His cunning tactics seek to undermine faith, disrupt relationships, and hinder spiritual growth. As saved individuals, our souls are secure, yet Satan endeavors to sow doubt, confusion, and discord in our walk with God.

Therefore, it is imperative to discern and resist the wiles of the enemy. Getting to know our adversary equips us to stay one step ahead, guarding against his subtle snares. Let us heed the admonition to not be fooled, to stand firm in faith, and to cultivate a deeper intimacy with God, undeterred by the adversary's deceitful schemes.

In a world fraught with confusion and deception, God's Word serves as a steadfast guide, illuminating the path to discernment and protection. Through verses like 1 Corinthians 14:33 and Ephesians 4:14-16, believers are urged to arm themselves with truth and unity, guarding against the cunning schemes of the enemy.

1 Corinthians 14:33

[33]For God is not the author of confusion, but of peace, as in all churches of the saints.

Ephesians 4:14-16

[14]That we henceforth be no more children, tossed to and fro, and carried about with every wind of doctrine, by the sleight of men, and cunning craftiness, whereby they lie in wait to deceive; [15]But speaking the truth in love, may grow up into him in all things, which is the head, even Christ: [16]From whom the whole body fitly joined together and compacted by that which every joint supplieth, according to the effectual working in the measure of every part, maketh increase of the body unto the edifying of itself in love.

Who will win in the end? Of course God will prevail!

I encourage you to pray for God's graceful guidance as you read, meditate on, and memorize the chosen scripture revealed to you by the Holy Spirit.

Genesis 1:1-4 | *Narrates the creation of the world by God. Some interpretations suggest that before the creation described in these verses, Satan, previously an angel of light, had already fallen from grace, resulting in the darkness present on the earth. This view aligns with the notion that darkness symbolizes Satan's presence and influence. However, the focus of these verses is on God's act of bringing light into existence, symbolizing His power over darkness and the beginning of creation.*

¹In the beginning God created the heaven and the earth. ²And the earth was without form, and void; and darkness was upon the face of the deep. And the Spirit of God moved upon the face of the waters. ³And God said, Let there be light: and there was light. ⁴And God saw the light, that it was good: and God divided the light from the darkness.

Genesis 3:1-14 | *Recounts the deception of Eve by the serpent, identified as Satan in later biblical interpretations. The serpent cunningly questions Eve about God's command regarding the fruit of the tree in the midst of the garden. Eve, deceived by the serpent's words, eats the fruit and shares it with Adam. Upon eating, their eyes are opened to their nakedness, and they hide from God's presence. When confronted by God, Adam blames Eve, and Eve blames the serpent. As a result of the deception, God curses the serpent above all animals, condemning it to crawl on its belly and eat dust for the rest of its days.*

¹Now the serpent was more subtil than any beast of the field which the Lord God had made. And he said unto the woman, Yea, hath God said, Ye shall not eat of every tree of the garden? ²And the woman said unto the serpent, We may eat of the fruit of the trees of the garden: ³But of the fruit of the tree which is in the midst of the garden, God hath said, Ye shall not eat of it, neither shall ye touch it, lest ye die. ⁴And the serpent said unto the woman, Ye shall not surely die: ⁵For God doth know that in the day ye eat thereof, then your eyes shall be opened, and ye shall be as gods, knowing good and evil. ⁶And when the woman saw that the tree was good for food, and that it was pleasant to the eyes, and a tree to be desired to make one wise, she took of the fruit thereof, and did eat, and gave also unto her husband with her; and he did eat. ⁷And the eyes of them both were opened, and they knew that they were naked; and they sewed fig leaves together, and made themselves aprons. ⁸And they heard the voice of the Lord God walking in the garden in the cool of the day: and Adam and his wife hid themselves from the presence of the Lord God amongst the trees of the garden. ⁹And the Lord God called unto Adam, and said unto him, Where art thou? ¹⁰And he said, I heard thy voice in the garden, and I was afraid, because I was naked; and I hid myself. ¹¹And he said, Who told thee that thou wast naked? Hast thou eaten of the tree, whereof I commanded thee that

thou shouldest not eat? ¹²And the man said, The woman whom thou gavest to be with me, she gave me of the tree, and I did eat. ¹³And the Lord God said unto the woman, What is this that thou hast done? And the woman said, The serpent beguiled me, and I did eat. ¹⁴And the Lord God said unto the serpent, Because thou hast done this, thou art cursed above all cattle, and above every beast of the field; upon thy belly shalt thou go, and dust shalt thou eat all the days of thy life:

Job 1 & 2 – Please take the time to read the book of Job.
The aforementioned chapters illustrate Satan's interaction with God, wherein he tests Job to assess the depth of Job's devotion and faithfulness to God.

Job 1:7 | *This verse explicitly depicts Satan's movement between earth and heaven, indicating a pattern of traversing back and forth. This imagery suggests that Satan is constantly moving about the earth, observing, influencing, and seeking opportunities to carry out his purposes. It portrays him as an active and persistent presence, seeking to exploit weaknesses and sow discord among humanity.*

⁷And the Lord said unto Satan, Whence comest thou? Then Satan answered the Lord, and said, From going to and fro in the earth, and from walking up and down in it.

Proverbs 12:6 | *This imagery implies that Satan, often associated with wickedness, uses deceitful words to lure people into believing falsehoods and ultimately being deceived. In contrast, the mouth of the upright, representing those who uphold righteousness and truth, serves to deliver others from such deception.*

⁶The words of the wicked are to lie in wait for blood: but the mouth of the upright shall deliver them.

Isaiah 14:12 | *The prophet addresses Lucifer, who is traditionally interpreted as a reference to Satan, and describes his fall from heaven. The imagery of Lucifer's descent from heaven depicts his rebellion against God and his subsequent expulsion from the divine realm. This verse underscores the consequences of pride and rebellion, portraying Satan's downfall as a significant event with far-reaching implications.*

¹²How art thou fallen from heaven, O Lucifer, son of the morning! how art thou cut down to the ground, which didst weaken the nations!

Jeremiah 9:3-5 | *The prophet describes a pervasive atmosphere of deceit and falsehood on earth. The people are depicted as using their tongues to spread lies and slander instead of seeking and upholding the truth. This passage highlights the prevalence of deception and the absence of genuine commitment to righteousness. It suggests that amidst the prevalence of falsehoods, God seeks those who are valiant for the truth, discerning between deceit and sincerity in their pursuit of His divine truth. These verses also talk about how there will be lies (from Satan) on earth to believe because God wants to know who will seek the truth...His truth.*

³And they bend their tongues like their bow for lies: but they are not valiant for the truth upon the earth; for they proceed from evil to evil, and they know not me, saith the Lord. ⁴Take ye heed every one of his neighbour, and trust ye not in any brother: for every brother will utterly supplant, and every neighbour will walk with slanders. ⁵And they will deceive every one his neighbour, and will not speak the truth: they have taught their tongue to speak lies, and weary themselves to commit iniquity.

Jeremiah 23:26 | *The prophet condemns false prophets who spread lies and deceit. The verse emphasizes the prevalence of falsehoods propagated by these prophets, suggesting that their words originate from the deceit within their own hearts. This passage underscores the insidious influence of deception, suggesting that Satan may be behind these lies, perpetuating falsehoods to lead people astray.*

²⁶How long shall this be in the heart of the prophets that prophesy lies? yea, they are prophets of the deceit of their own heart;

Jeremiah 27:10 & 15 | *The prophet warns about false prophets who speak lies in the name of God. These lies lead people astray, causing them to drift further from God's truth and ultimately face destruction. The verses emphasize the grave consequences of believing and following these falsehoods, suggesting that such deception can lead to spiritual death and eternal separation from God.*

¹⁰For they prophesy a lie unto you, to remove you far from your land; and that I should drive you out, and ye should perish. ¹⁵For I have not sent them, saith the Lord, yet they prophesy a lie in my name; that I might drive you out, and that ye might perish, ye, and the prophets that prophesy unto you.

Zechariah 3:1-2 | *The prophet describes a vision where Joshua the high priest stands before the angel of the Lord, with Satan positioned at his right hand to accuse him. This scene depicts Satan's ongoing role as an adversary, opposing the righteous before God. However, the Lord rebukes Satan, asserting His authority and affirming His choice of Jerusalem. The imagery suggests the constant spiritual battle between good and evil, with God ultimately triumphing over Satan's accusations.*

¹And he shewed me Joshua the high priest standing before the angel of the Lord, and Satan standing at his right hand to resist him. ²And the Lord said unto Satan, The Lord rebuke thee, O Satan; even the Lord that hath chosen Jerusalem rebuke thee: is not this a brand plucked out of the fire?

Matthew 4:1-11 | *Jesus is led by the Spirit into the wilderness to be tempted by the devil after fasting for forty days and nights. Satan attempts to lure Jesus into sin by tempting Him with worldly desires and power. However, Jesus responds to each temptation by quoting scripture, demonstrating His reliance on the Word of God and His refusal to yield to temptation. Despite the devil's persistent efforts, Jesus* *remains steadfast and ultimately commands Satan to leave, after which angels come to minister to Him. This passage illustrates Jesus' victory over temptation and the power of relying on the Word of God to overcome spiritual challenges.*

¹Then was Jesus led up of the Spirit into the wilderness to be tempted of the devil. ²And when he had fasted forty days and forty nights, he was afterward an hungred. ³And when the tempter came to him, he said, If thou be the Son of God, command that these stones be made bread. ⁴But he answered and said, It is written, Man shall not live by bread alone, but by every word that proceedeth out of the mouth of God. ⁵Then the devil taketh him up into the holy city, and setteth him on a pinnacle of the temple, ⁶And saith unto him, If thou be the Son of God, cast thyself down: for it is written, He shall give his angels charge concerning thee: and in their hands they shall bear thee up, lest at any time thou dash thy foot against a stone. ⁷Jesus said unto him, It is written again, Thou shalt not tempt the Lord thy God. ⁸Again, the devil taketh him up into an exceeding high mountain, and sheweth him all the kingdoms of the world, and the glory of them; ⁹And saith unto him, All these things will I give thee, if thou wilt fall down and worship me. ¹⁰Then saith Jesus unto him, Get thee hence, Satan: for it is written, Thou shalt worship the Lord thy God, and him only shalt thou serve. ¹¹Then the devil leaveth him, and, behold, angels came and ministered unto him.

Matthew 12:26-30 | *This states that Satan has a kingdom, which is the earth. Jesus addresses the Pharisees' accusation that He casts out demons by the power of Satan. Jesus explains that Satan's kingdom would be divided if he were to oppose himself, indicating that Satan indeed has a kingdom. However, Jesus asserts that His ability to cast out demons by the Spirit of God signifies the arrival of the kingdom of God. He uses the analogy of binding a strong man to illustrate His authority over Satan and his kingdom. Ultimately, Jesus emphasizes the importance of aligning oneself with Him, highlighting the spiritual battle between good and evil and the necessity of choosing sides.*

²⁶And if Satan cast out Satan, he is divided against himself; how shall then his kingdom stand? ²⁷And if I by Beelzebub cast out devils, by whom do your children cast them out? therefore they shall be your judges. ²⁸But if I cast out devils by the Spirit of God, then the kingdom of God is come unto you. ²⁹Or else how can one enter into a strong man's house, and spoil his goods, except he first bind the strong man? and then he will spoil his house. ³⁰He that is not with me is against me; and he that gathereth not with me scattereth abroad.

Matthew 16:23-27 | *Jesus rebukes Peter for his earthly-mindedness, identifying Satan's influence behind Peter's words. Jesus then teaches his disciples about the cost of discipleship, emphasizing the need for self-denial, taking up one's cross, and following Him. He contrasts worldly gain with the eternal value of one's soul, highlighting the importance of prioritizing spiritual matters over temporal concerns. Jesus concludes* *by affirming His eventual return in glory, promising to reward each person according to their deeds. This passage underscores the call to wholehearted commitment to Christ and the eternal significance of following Him.*

[23]But he turned, and said unto Peter, Get thee behind me, Satan: thou art an offence unto me: for thou savourest not the things that be of God, but those that be of men. [24]Then said Jesus unto his disciples, If any man will come after me, let him deny himself, and take up his cross, and follow me. [25]For whosoever will save his life shall lose it: and whosoever will lose his life for my sake shall find it. [26]For what is a man profited, if he shall gain the whole world, and lose his own soul? or what shall a man give in exchange for his soul? [27]For the Son of man shall come in the glory of his Father with his angels; and then he shall reward every man according to his works.

Mark 1:13 | *Jesus undergoes temptation by Satan during His forty days in the wilderness. Despite being tested, Jesus remains steadfast and relies on the Word of God to resist temptation. The presence of wild beasts symbolizes the harshness of the wilderness, while the angels ministering to Him afterward highlights God's provision and care even in times of trial. This passage illustrates Jesus' victory over temptation and His reliance on divine strength during moments of testing.*

[13]And he was there in the wilderness forty days, tempted of Satan; and was with the wild beasts; and the angels ministered unto him.

Mark 3:23-27 | *Jesus uses parables to explain that Satan's kingdom, represented by the earth, cannot stand if it is divided against itself. He illustrates this by stating that a kingdom or house divided against itself cannot endure. By referencing Satan's kingdom, Jesus implies that Satan exercises authority over the world. Additionally, Jesus describes how a strong man must be bound before his house can be plundered, suggesting that Satan is the strong man whose authority must be overcome in order to thwart his influence on earth. This passage underscores the reality of spiritual warfare and the need for Jesus to assert His authority over the dominion of darkness.*

[23]And he called them unto him, and said unto them in parables, How can Satan cast out Satan? [24]And if a kingdom be divided against itself, that kingdom cannot stand. [25]And if a house be divided against itself, that house cannot stand. [26]And if Satan rise up against himself, and be divided, he cannot stand, but hath an end. [27]No man can enter into a strong man's house, and spoil his goods, except he will first bind the strong man; and then he will spoil his house.

Mark 4:1-25 – Read entire passage but stop and meditate on verse 15.
Jesus teaches a crowd using parables, including the Parable of the Sower. In verse 15, Jesus explains that when the Word of God is sown along the wayside (symbolizing those who hear but don't understand), Satan comes immediately to snatch away the Word from their hearts. This verse illustrates how Satan actively seeks to prevent people from receiving and retaining the truth of God's Word, highlighting the importance of guarding one's heart and remaining vigilant against spiritual attacks.

¹And he began again to teach by the sea side: and there was gathered unto him a great multitude, so that he entered into a ship, and sat in the sea; and the whole multitude was by the sea on the land. ²And he taught them many things by parables, and said unto them in his doctrine, ³Hearken; Behold, there went out a sower to sow: ⁴And it came to pass, as he sowed, some fell by the way side, and the fowls of the air came and devoured it up. ⁵And some fell on stony ground, where it had not much earth; and immediately it sprang up, because it had no depth of earth: ⁶But when the sun was up, it was scorched; and because it had no root, it withered away. ⁷And some fell among thorns, and the thorns grew up, and choked it, and it yielded no fruit. ⁸And other fell on good ground, and did yield fruit that sprang up and increased; and brought forth, some thirty, and some sixty, and some an hundred. ⁹And he said unto them, He that hath ears to hear, let him hear. ¹⁰And when he was alone, they that were about him with the twelve asked of him the parable. ¹¹And he said unto them, Unto you it is given to know the mystery of the kingdom of God: but unto them that are without, all these things are done in parables: ¹²That seeing they may see, and not perceive; and hearing they may hear, and not understand; lest at any time they should be converted, and their sins should be forgiven them. ¹³And he said unto them, Know ye not this parable? and how then will ye know all parables? ¹⁴The sower soweth the word. ¹⁵And these are they by the way side, where the word is sown; but when they have heard, Satan cometh immediately, and taketh away the word that was sown in their hearts. ¹⁶And these are they likewise which are sown on stony ground; who, when they have heard the word, immediately receive it with gladness; ¹⁷And have no root in themselves, and so endure but for a time: afterward, when affliction or persecution ariseth for the word's sake, immediately they are offended. ¹⁸And these are they which are sown among thorns; such as hear the word, ¹⁹And the cares of this world, and the deceitfulness of riches, and the lusts of other things entering in, choke the word, and it becometh unfruitful. ²⁰And these are they which are sown on good ground; such as hear the word, and receive it, and bring forth fruit, some thirtyfold, some sixty, and some an hundred. ²¹And he said unto them, Is a candle brought to be put under a bushel, or under a bed? and not to be set on a candlestick? ²²For there is nothing hid, which shall not be manifested; neither was any thing kept secret, but that it should come abroad. ²³If any man have ears to hear, let him hear. ²⁴And he said unto them, Take heed what ye hear: with what measure ye mete, it shall be measured to you: and unto you that hear shall more be given. ²⁵For he that hath, to him shall be given: and he that hath not, from him shall be taken even that which he hath.

Mark 8:33 | *Jesus rebukes Peter after he expresses resistance to Jesus' prediction of His suffering and death. By addressing Peter as "Satan," Jesus is not implying that Peter is literally Satan, but rather rebuking the mindset and influence behind Peter's words. This verse highlights Satan's deceptive tactics, as Peter's words reflect a mindset aligned with human desires rather than God's purposes. It underscores how Satan can subtly influence people to prioritize worldly concerns over spiritual truths, seeking to exert control and authority over them.*

³³But when he had turned about and looked on his disciples, he rebuked Peter, saying, Get thee behind me, Satan: for thou savourest not the things that be of God, but the things that be of men.

Luke 4:8 | *Satan tempts Jesus by offering Him authority over all the kingdoms of the world in exchange for worship. However, Jesus responds by quoting scripture, specifically Deuteronomy 6:13, reaffirming the command to worship and serve only God. This verse illustrates Jesus' unwavering commitment in the obedience to God's Word, even in the face of temptation from Satan. It highlights the power of scripture as a weapon against temptation and the importance of prioritizing God above all else.*

⁸And Jesus answered and said unto him, Get thee behind me, Satan: for it is written, Thou shalt worship the Lord thy God, and him only shalt thou serve.

Luke 10:17-18 | *The seventy disciples report back to Jesus with joy, sharing their success in casting out demons. Jesus responds by acknowledging that He saw Satan fall from heaven like lightning. This statement suggests that Satan's fall from heaven is a past event witnessed by Jesus. It underscores Jesus' authority over the demonic realm and affirms the defeat of Satan's power through the disciples' ministry empowered by Jesus' name.*

¹⁷And the seventy returned again with joy, saying, Lord, even the devils are subject unto us through thy name. ¹⁸And he said unto them, I beheld Satan as lightning fall from heaven.

Luke 13:16 | *Jesus refers to a woman who had been bound by Satan for eighteen years. This verse illustrates the oppressive influence of Satan, who had afflicted the woman with physical infirmity. Jesus' statement highlights His authority and ability to deliver individuals from the bondage imposed by Satan, emphasizing the importance of liberation from spiritual oppression, even on the Sabbath day.*

¹⁶And ought not this woman, being a daughter of Abraham, whom Satan hath bound, lo, these eighteen years, be loosed from this bond on the sabbath day?

Luke 22:3 | *It is mentioned that Satan entered into Judas Iscariot, one of Jesus' disciples. This verse highlights how Satan influenced Judas to betray Jesus, illustrating the extent of Satan's manipulation and deception. It underscores the spiritual conflict between good and evil, revealing Satan's relentless efforts to undermine Jesus' ministry and disrupt God's plan of salvation.*

³Then entered Satan into Judas surnamed Iscariot, being of the number of the twelve.

John 13:27 | *It is depicted that Satan entered into Judas Iscariot, one of Jesus' disciples. This verse demonstrates how Satan influenced Judas to betray Jesus, symbolizing the spiritual conflict between good and evil. It highlights the vulnerability of individuals to Satanic influence and underscores the importance of remaining vigilant against spiritual deception.*

27And after the sop Satan entered into him. Then said Jesus unto him, That thou doest, do quickly.

Acts 5:3 | *Peter confronts Ananias, questioning why Satan has filled his heart to lie to the Holy Spirit and withhold part of the proceeds from the sale of his property. This verse illustrates how Satan can influence individuals to act deceitfully and against God's will. It emphasizes the seriousness of yielding to Satanic influence and the importance of integrity and honesty in one's actions before God.*

3But Peter said, Ananias, why hath Satan filled thine heart to lie to the Holy Ghost, and to keep back part of the price of the land?

Acts 26:18 | *This verse connects that Satan is also called darkness in Genesis 1 and how Satan does have power on this earth (if people let him). It is expressed that the mission of Paul is to open the eyes of people, leading them from darkness to light, and from the power of Satan to God. This verse underscores Satan's role as the force behind spiritual darkness and emphasizes the power he holds over those who are not aligned with God. However, it also highlights the transformative power of faith in Jesus Christ, which enables individuals to break free from Satan's influence and receive forgiveness of sins, ultimately securing an inheritance among the sanctified.*

18To open their eyes, and to turn them from darkness to light, and from the power of Satan unto God, that they may receive forgiveness of sins, and inheritance among them which are sanctified by faith that is in me.

Romans 1:25 | *It is depicted that people exchanged the truth of God for a lie, worshiping and serving created things rather than the Creator. This verse illustrates how human beings can distort and misinterpret God's truth, replacing it with falsehoods. It suggests that Satan's influence leads to the alteration and corruption of God's Word, ultimately causing confusion and misguidance among people.*

25Who changed the truth of God into a lie, and worshiped and served the creature more than the Creator, who is blessed for ever. Amen.

Romans 16:20 | *Asserts that God, the God of peace, will soon crush Satan under the feet of believers. This verse speaks to the ultimate victory of God over Satan and the assurance of triumph for those who stand firm in their faith. It provides comfort and encouragement to believers, emphasizing the power and authority of God over evil forces.*

20And the God of peace shall bruise Satan under your feet shortly. The grace of our Lord Jesus Christ be with you. Amen.

1 Corinthians 5:5 | *It is suggested to hand over an individual to Satan for the destruction of their flesh, with the hope that their spirit may be saved on the day of the Lord Jesus. This verse implies a severe disciplinary action, possibly excommunication from the church, to address the individual's sinful behavior. The goal is ultimately for the individual to repent and be saved, even if it requires facing the consequences of their actions.*

⁵To deliver such an one unto Satan for the destruction of the flesh, that the spirit may be saved in the day of the Lord Jesus.

1 Corinthians 7:5 | *Believers are urged not to defraud one another in their marital relationships, except by mutual agreement for a limited time devoted to fasting and prayer. The verse warns against allowing Satan to tempt them due to lack of self-control or sexual immorality. It underscores the importance of maintaining fidelity and mutual respect within marriages to guard against Satanic influence and uphold the sanctity of the marital bond.*

⁵Defraud ye not one the other, except it be with consent for a time, that ye may give yourselves to fasting and prayer; and come together again, that Satan tempt you not for your incontinency.

2 Corinthians 2:11 | *Believers are cautioned against being ignorant of Satan's schemes, lest he gains an advantage over them. This verse emphasizes the importance of understanding and being aware of Satan's tactics, as ignorance can leave individuals vulnerable to his deceitful influences. By recognizing and discerning his strategies, believers can resist his schemes and stand firm in their faith.*

¹¹Lest Satan should get an advantage of us: for we are not ignorant of his devices.

2 Corinthians 11:14-15 | *It's highlighted that Satan can masquerade as an angel of light, portraying himself as something good and righteous, even though he is not. This verse warns that Satan's agents may also appear as ministers of righteousness, but their true intentions and actions will ultimately reveal their deceitful nature. It underscores the deceptive tactics employed by Satan to deceive and mislead people, emphasizing the need for discernment and vigilance in recognizing his false guise.*

¹⁴And no marvel; for Satan himself is transformed into an angel of light. ¹⁵Therefore it is no great thing if his ministers also be transformed as the ministers of righteousness; whose end shall be according to their works.

1 Thessalonians 2:18 | *Paul indicates that he and his companions intended to visit the Thessalonian believers on multiple occasions, but they were prevented from doing so by Satan. This verse illustrates how Satan actively obstructs and interferes with the plans and endeavors of believers, seeking to hinder their efforts in spreading the Gospel and nurturing fellow believers. It serves as a reminder of the spiritual warfare that believers face and the need for perseverance and reliance on God's strength in overcoming such obstacles.*

[18]Wherefore we would have come unto you, even I Paul, once and again; but Satan hindered us.

2 Thessalonians 2:9 | *It's highlighted that there will be a figure whose arrival is accompanied by the deceptive workings of Satan, manifesting with great power, signs, and deceptive miracles. This verse emphasizes the presence of spiritual deception and the influence of Satan on the earth, leading up to the eventual return of Jesus. It underscores the need for discernment and vigilance among believers to recognize and resist such falsehoods in anticipation of Christ's return.*

[9]Even him, whose coming is after the working of Satan with all power and signs and lying wonders,

1 Timothy 1:20 | *Paul mentions two individuals, Hymenaeus and Alexander, whom he delivered to Satan as a form of disciplinary action. This action was aimed at teaching them not to blaspheme. While the verse doesn't explicitly state that Satan takes lives, it reflects a severe disciplinary measure taken by Paul within the context of the early Christian community. It suggests a form of spiritual discipline wherein these individuals were temporarily handed over to Satan's influence, possibly to experience the consequences of their actions and to learn from them.*

[20]Of whom is Hymenaeus and Alexander; whom I have delivered unto Satan, that they may learn not to blaspheme.

1 Timothy 5:15 | *It is stated that some individuals have already turned away from the path of righteousness and aligned themselves with Satan. This verse underscores the reality of spiritual opposition and the temptation for individuals to deviate from the truth, choosing instead to follow the deceitful ways of Satan. It serves as a warning against the allure of evil influences and the importance of remaining steadfast in one's faith.*

[15]For some are already turned aside after Satan.

1 Peter 5:8 | *Believers are urged to maintain sobriety and vigilance because the devil, likened to a roaring lion, is actively seeking whom he can devour. This verse emphasizes the constant spiritual warfare believers face and the need to be alert to Satan's schemes. By remaining vigilant and grounded in faith, believers can protect themselves from falling prey to the enemy's tactics.*

[8]Be sober, be vigilant; because your adversary the devil, as a roaring lion, walketh about, seeking whom he may devour:

Revelation 2:2 & 9-24 | *Read entire passage but stop and meditate on verses 2, 13, & 24. Various churches are addressed, each with commendations and admonitions. Despite facing poverty and tribulations, these believers are rich in faith and labor diligently for God. They are commended for their perseverance and discernment against false teachings. However, some are rebuked for tolerating false doctrines and immoral behavior. Despite challenges, those who remain faithful are promised rewards and protection from spiritual harm. These verses highlight God's awareness of His people's struggles and His expectation for them to remain steadfast in faith.*

²I know thy works, and thy labour, and thy patience, and how thou canst not bear them which are evil: and thou hast tried them which say they are apostles, and are not, and hast found them liars: ⁹I know thy works, and tribulation, and poverty, (but thou art rich) and I know the blasphemy of them which say they are Jews, and are not, but are the synagogue of Satan. ¹⁰Fear none of those things which thou shalt suffer: behold, the devil shall cast some of you into prison, that ye may be tried; and ye shall have tribulation ten days: be thou faithful unto death, and I will give thee a crown of life. ¹¹He that hath an ear, let him hear what the Spirit saith unto the churches; He that overcometh shall not be hurt of the second death. ¹²And to the angel of the church in Pergamos write; These things saith he which hath the sharp sword with two edges; ¹³I know thy works, and where thou dwellest, even where Satan's seat is: and thou holdest fast my name, and hast not denied my faith, even in those days wherein Antipas was my faithful martyr, who was slain among you, where Satan dwelleth. ¹⁴But I have a few things against thee, because thou hast there them that hold the doctrine of Balaam, who taught Balac to cast a stumblingblock before the children of Israel, to eat things sacrificed unto idols, and to commit fornication. ¹⁵So hast thou also them that hold the doctrine of the Nicolaitanes, which thing I hate. ¹⁶Repent; or else I will come unto thee quickly, and will fight against them with the sword of my mouth. ¹⁷He that hath an ear, let him hear what the Spirit saith unto the churches; To him that overcometh will I give to eat of the hidden manna, and will give him a white stone, and in the stone a new name written, which no man knoweth saving he that receiveth it. ¹⁸And unto the angel of the church in Thyatira write; These things saith the Son of God, who hath his eyes like unto a flame of fire, and his feet are like fine brass; ¹⁹I know thy works, and charity, and service, and faith, and thy patience, and thy works; and the last to be more than the first. ²⁰Notwithstanding I have a few things against thee, because thou sufferest that woman Jezebel, which calleth herself a prophetess, to teach and to seduce my servants to commit fornication, and to eat things sacrificed unto idols. ²¹And I gave her space to repent of her fornication; and she repented not. ²²Behold, I will cast her into a bed, and them that commit adultery with her into great tribulation, except they repent of their deeds. ²³And I will kill her children with death; and all the churches shall know that I am he which searcheth the reins and hearts: and I will give unto every

one of you according to your works. [24]But unto you I say, and unto the rest in Thyatira, as many as have not this doctrine, and which have not known the depths of Satan, as they speak; I will put upon you none other burden.

Revelation 3:9 | *Reassures believers of God's love and vindication. Despite facing opposition and falsehoods from those who claim to be faithful but are not, God promises to expose their deceit and demonstrate His love for His true followers by bringing them recognition and honor.*

[9]Behold, I will make them of the synagogue of Satan, which say they are Jews, and are not, but do lie; behold, I will make them to come and worship before thy feet, and to know that I have loved thee.

Revelation 12:9-10 | *Depicts the expulsion of Satan and his followers from heaven. Identified as the great dragon, old serpent, and Devil, Satan is described as the deceiver of the world. The passage celebrates this event, declaring the arrival of salvation, strength, and the reign of God's kingdom. It signifies the defeat of Satan as the accuser of believers, who continuously brought accusations against them before God.*

[9]And the great dragon was cast out, that old serpent, called the Devil, and Satan, which deceiveth the whole world: he was cast out into the earth, and his angels were cast out with him. [10]And I heard a loud voice saying in heaven, Now is come salvation, and strength, and the kingdom of our God, and the power of his Christ: for the accuser of our brethren is cast down, which accused them before our God day and night.

Revelation 20:2-8 | *Portrays the binding of Satan by God for a thousand years. The passage describes Satan's confinement in the bottomless pit, sealed to prevent deception of nations until the thousand years pass. During this time, believers who were martyred for Jesus reign with Christ. Following this period, Satan is released temporarily to deceive nations, culminating in a great battle against God's people.*

[2]And he laid hold on the dragon, that old serpent, which is the Devil, and Satan, and bound him a thousand years, [3]And cast him into the bottomless pit, and shut him up, and set a seal upon him, that he should deceive the nations no more, till the thousand years should be fulfilled: and after that he must be loosed a little season. [4]And I saw thrones, and they sat upon them, and judgment was given unto them: and I saw the souls of them that were beheaded for the witness of Jesus, and for the word of God, and which had not worshipped the beast, neither his image, neither had received his mark upon their foreheads, or in their hands; and they lived and reigned with Christ a thousand years. [5]But the rest of the dead lived not again until the thousand years were finished. This is the first resurrection. [6]Blessed and holy is he that hath part in the first resurrection: on such the second death hath no power, but they shall be priests of God and of Christ, and shall reign with him a thousand years. [7]And when the thousand years are expired, Satan shall be loosed out of his prison, [8]And shall

go out to deceive the nations which are in the four quarters of the earth, Gog, and Magog, to gather them together to battle: the number of whom is as the sand of the sea.

Revelation 22:16 | *Emphasizes Jesus' identity, where He declares Himself as the root and offspring of David, highlighting His lineage and messianic role. Additionally, He refers to Himself as the bright and morning star, symbolizing His radiance and role as a guiding light for humanity.*

[16]I Jesus have sent mine angel to testify unto you these things in the churches. I am the root and the offspring of David, and the bright and morning star.

*A collection of scriptures by **Tonya Truster***

NOTES

_____

_____

_____

_____

_____

_____

_____

_____

_____

_____

_____

_____

_____

_____

_____

_____

_____

_____

_____

_____

_____

_____

_____

_____

_____

_____

_____

_____

_____

NOTES

NOTES

TRUST GOD'S PROMISES

Trusting in God's promises is the cornerstone of a faithful life. Throughout the Bible, we are encouraged to rely on God in every aspect of our lives, from seeking His guidance through prayer to understanding His plan revealed in His Word. As believers, we are called not only to talk with God but also to rely on Him completely, acknowledging His sovereignty and wisdom. These verses serve as a road map for navigating life's challenges with unwavering faith, knowing that God's promises are true and His love for us is everlasting. Let us delve into these passages to glean wisdom, find solace, and strengthen our trust in the One who holds our future in His hands.

I encourage you to pray for God's graceful guidance as you read, meditate on, and memorize the chosen scripture revealed to you by the Holy Spirit.

T alk to God
R ely on God
U nderstand God's Plan
S tudy God's Word
T ell others about God

Proverbs 3:5-6
⁵Trust in the Lord with all thine heart; and lean not unto thine own understanding. ⁶In all thy ways acknowledge him, and he shall direct thy paths.

1 Thessalonians 5:17
¹⁷Pray without ceasing.

Philippians 4:6
⁶Be careful for nothing; but in every thing by prayer and supplication with thanksgiving let your requests be made known unto God.

1 Peter 5:6-7
⁶Humble yourselves therefore under the mighty hand of God, that he may exalt you in due time: ⁷Casting all your care upon him; for he careth for you.

Mark 10:27
²⁷And Jesus looking upon them saith, With men it is impossible, but not with God: for with God all things are possible.

James 1:22-24
²²But be ye doers of the word, and not hearers only, deceiving your own selves. ²³For if any be a hearer of the word, and not a doer, he is like unto a man beholding his natural face in a glass: ²⁴For he beholdeth himself, and goeth his way, and straightway forgetteth what manner of man he was.

James 1:17
¹⁷Every good gift and every perfect gift is from above, and cometh down from the Father of lights, with whom is no variableness, neither shadow of turning.

Romans 12:2-3
²And be not conformed to this world: but be ye transformed by the renewing of your mind, that ye may prove what is that good, and acceptable, and perfect, will of God. ³For I say, through the grace given unto me, to every man that is among you, not to think of himself more highly than he ought to think; but to think soberly, according as God hath dealt to every man the measure of faith.

Proverbs 11:1-2
¹A false balance is abomination to the LORD: but a just weight is his delight. ²When pride cometh, then cometh shame: but with the lowly is wisdom.

Proverbs 16:18
¹⁸Pride goeth before destruction, and an haughty spirit before a fall.

Galatians 5:22-23
²²But the fruit of the Spirit is love, joy, peace, longsuffering, gentleness, goodness, faith, ²³Meekness, temperance: against such there is no law.

James 1:13-14
¹³Let no man say when he is tempted, I am tempted of God: for God cannot be tempted with evil, neither tempteth he any man: ¹⁴But every man is tempted, when he is drawn away of his own lust, and enticed.

Psalm 118:6
⁶The LORD is on my side; I will not fear: what can man do unto me?

Psalm 96:4
⁴For the LORD is great, and greatly to be praised: he is to be feared above all gods.

Proverbs 13:1
¹A wise son heareth his father's instruction: but a scorner heareth not rebuke.

Proverbs 17:1
¹Better is a dry morsel, and quietness therewith, than an house full of sacrifices with strife.

A collection of scriptures by **Tonya Truster**

Proverbs 19:1

¹Better is the poor that walketh in his integrity, than he that is perverse in his lips, and is a fool.

1 Peter 5:8

⁸Be sober, be vigilant; because your adversary the devil, as a roaring lion, walketh about, seeking whom he may devour:

Ecclesiastes 3:1-11

¹To everything there is a season, and a time to every purpose under the heaven: ²A time to be born, and a time to die; a time to plant, and a time to pluck up that which is planted; ³A time to kill, and a time to heal; a time to break down, and a time to build up; ⁴A time to weep, and a time to laugh; a time to mourn, and a time to dance; ⁵A time to cast away stones, and a time to gather stones together; a time to embrace, and a time to refrain from embracing; ⁶A time to get, and a time to lose; a time to keep, and a time to cast away; ⁷A time to rend, and a time to sew; a time to keep silence, and a time to speak; ⁸A time to love, and a time to hate; a time of war, and a time of peace. ⁹What profit hath he that worketh in that wherein he laboureth? ¹⁰I have seen the travail, which God hath given to the sons of men to be exercised in it. ¹¹He hath made everything beautiful in his time: also he hath set the world in their heart, so that no man can find out the work that God maketh from the beginning to the end.

Numbers 32:23

²³But if ye will not do so, behold, ye have sinned against the LORD: and be sure your sin will find you out.

Romans 8:28

²⁸And we know that all things work together for good to them that love God, to them who are the called according to his purpose.

Matthew 5:14

¹⁴Ye are the light of the world. A city that is set on an hill cannot be hid.

Matthew 7:11

¹¹If ye then, being evil, know how to give good gifts unto your children, how much more shall your Father which is in heaven give good things to them that ask him?

Philippians 4:13

¹³I can do all things through Christ which strengtheneth me.

Isaiah 40:31

³¹But they that wait upon the LORD shall renew their strength; they shall mount up with wings as eagles; they shall run, and not be weary; and they shall walk, and not faint.

Psalm 119:10-11

[10]With my whole heart have I sought thee: O let me not wander from thy commandments. [11]Thy word have I hid in mine heart, that I might not sin against thee.

Psalm 102:1-2

[1]Hear my prayer, O LORD, and let my cry come unto thee. [2]Hide not thy face from me in the day when I am in trouble; incline thine ear unto me: in the day when I call answer me speedily.

Psalm 100:4-5

[4]Enter into his gates with thanksgiving, and into his courts with praise: be thankful unto him, and bless his name. [5]For the LORD is good; his mercy is everlasting; and his truth endureth to all generations.

  A collection of scriptures by **Tonya Truster**

Psalm 86:7
[7]In the day of my trouble I will call upon thee: for thou wilt answer me.

Psalm 73:28
[28]But it is good for me to draw near to God: I have put my trust in the Lord GOD, that I may declare all thy works.

Psalm 71:1 & 8
[1]In thee, O LORD, do I put my trust: let me never be put to confusion. [8]Let my mouth be filled with thy praise and with thy honour all the day.

Psalm 62:5-6
[5]My soul, wait thou only upon God; for my expectation is from him. [6]He only is my rock and my salvation: he is my defence; I shall not be moved.

Psalm 56:10-11
[10]In God will I praise his word: in the LORD will I praise his word. [11]In God have I put my trust: I will not be afraid what man can do unto me.

Psalm 51:12
[12]Restore unto me the joy of thy salvation; and uphold me with thy free spirit.

Psalm 46:1
[1]God is our refuge and strength, a very present help in trouble.

Psalm 46:10
[10]Be still, and know that I am God: I will be exalted among the heathen, I will be exalted in the earth.

Psalm 40:1
[1]I waited patiently for the LORD; and he inclined unto me, and heard my cry.

Psalm 37:23
[23]The steps of a good man are ordered by the LORD: and he delighteth in his way.

Psalm 31:3
[3]For thou art my rock and my fortress; therefore for thy name's sake lead me, and guide me.

Psalm 5:3
[3]My voice shalt thou hear in the morning, O LORD; in the morning will I direct my prayer unto thee, and will look up.

Luke 1:37
[37]For with God nothing shall be impossible.

Colossians 3:1-2

[1]If ye then be risen with Christ, seek those things which are above, where Christ sitteth on the right hand of God. [2]Set your affection on things above, not on things on the earth.

Proverbs 6:16-19

[16]These six things doth the LORD hate: yea, seven are an abomination unto him: [17]A proud look, a lying tongue, and hands that shed innocent blood, [18]An heart that deviseth wicked imaginations, feet that be swift in running to mischief, [19]A false witness that speaketh lies, and he that soweth discord among brethren.

Psalm 71:1

[1]In thee, O Lord, do I put my trust: let me never be put to confusion.

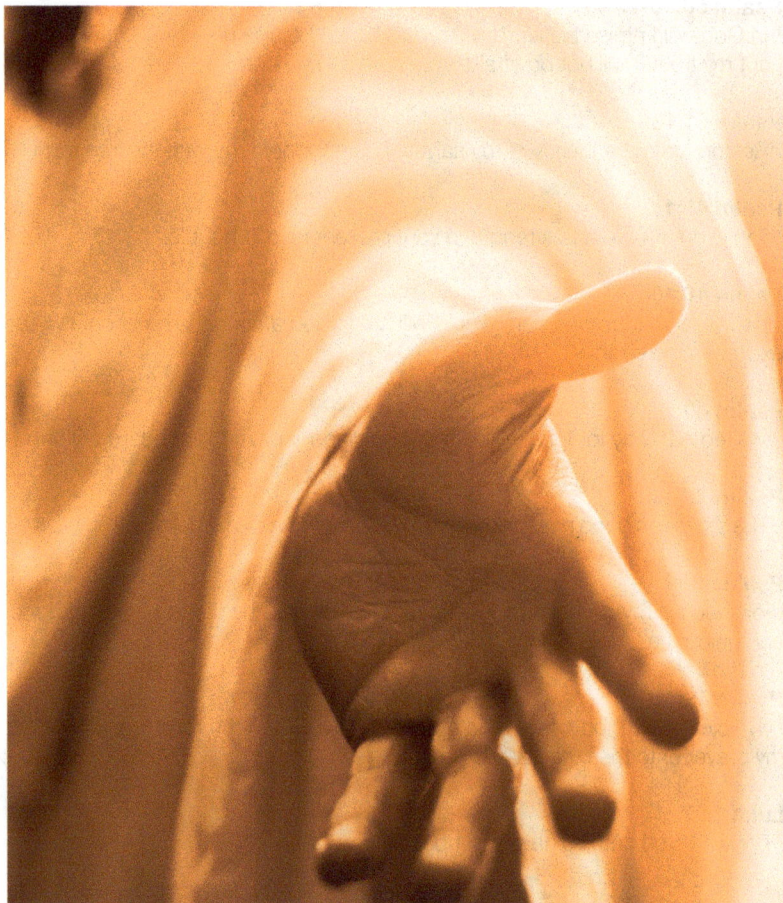

A collection of scriptures by **Tonya Truster**

Notes

NOTES

A collection of scriptures by **Tonya Truster**

NOTES

Author's Bio

Tonya Truster is a first-time published author with a lifelong passion for education and a deep love for the Bible. With over three decades of experience as an educator, Tonya has dedicated her career to inspiring and empowering students to reach their full potential.

Beyond the classroom, Tonya has spent over 30 years delving into the pages of the Bible, studying its teachings and uncovering its timeless wisdom. Her journey of faith has led her to participate in numerous Bible studies, including discipleship programs, where she has both learned and shared her knowledge with others. Tonya has also devoted herself to mentoring women and couples, guiding them on their spiritual journeys through one-on-one discipleship and group settings.

In addition to her commitment to studying and teaching the Bible, Tonya is actively involved in her local church community. She has taught Sunday school for youth, organized and led various women's Bible studies, and participated in Christian retreats aimed at deepening her understanding of scripture and fostering spiritual growth.

Through her debut book, Tonya aims to share her passion for the Bible and its transformative power with a wider audience. Drawing on her years of experience as both an educator and a dedicated student of scripture, Tonya offers readers a rich tapestry of insights and reflections to inspire and encourage them on their own spiritual journeys. Tonya has created an inspirational community Facebook page called Live Life, Love Life (Live the Life You Love. Love the Life You Live).

Tonya resides in Raymore, Missouri, with her husband, children, and grandchildren, where she continues to pursue her passion for education and faith. Connect with Tonya on her community Live Life, Love Life Facebook page or reach out via email at ttruster88@gmail.com.

www.ingramcontent.com/pod-product-compliance
Lightning Source LLC
Chambersburg PA
CBHW070254290326
41930CB00041B/2521